A Sense of Balance

JOHN HOWARD

A Sense of Balance

HarperCollins*Publishers*

HarperCollins*Publishers*
Australia • Brazil • Canada • France • Germany • Holland • India
Italy • Japan • Mexico • New Zealand • Poland • Spain • Sweden
Switzerland • United Kingdom • United States of America

HarperCollins acknowledges the Traditional Custodians
of the land upon which we live and work, and pays respect
to Elders past and present.

First published in Australia in 2022
by HarperCollins*Publishers* Australia Pty Limited
Gadigal Country
Level 13, 201 Elizabeth Street, Sydney NSW 2000
ABN 36 009 913 517
harpercollins.com.au

A catalogue record for this book is available from the National Library of Australia.

ISBN 978 1 4607 6262 2 (hardback)
ISBN 978 1 4607 1523 9 (ebook)
ISBN 978 1 4607 4469 7 (audiobook)

Cover design by HarperCollins Design Studio
Cover photography by Nic Walker
Typeset in Sabon LT Std by Kirby Jones
Printed and bound in Australia by McPherson's Printing Group

To my grandchildren, with the hope that Australia is as good to you as it has been to me

CONTENTS

INTRODUCTION

Australia has been kind to me, as it has to almost all who have been born in this blessed country, or have chosen to live here.

It is not white triumphalism to celebrate 'The Australian Achievement'. That was the designation assigned by the Fraser Government in 1981 to the bicentennial celebrations due to take place in 1988. It was a way of expressing quiet pride in what our nation had become: an essentially classless, economically self-reliant, wholly independent liberal democracy. A nation that sat comfortably at an intersection of history, geography and culture: profoundly Western in its civilisational background; increasingly immersed in the politics and economics of its immediate neighbourhood; warmly embracing its relationship with its major ally the United States, but always a citizen of the world that had long practised an open and non-discriminatory immigration policy. With the passage of time, I have grown ever more comfortable with 'The Australian Achievement' as a positive and eloquent, yet not overblown, description of our nation.

Yet in 1988, Australia still struggled to find the right way to honourably place its Aboriginal and Torres Strait Islander people within the mainstream of the nation. There was a largely united view that the First Australians were a disadvantaged group, and that more had to be done to remedy this. They had suffered prejudice and discrimination, which represented the greatest blemish in our national story. There were those who subscribed to what I would later call 'practical reconciliation'. Their focus was on improving the educational, health and housing opportunities for Indigenous people, thereby achieving a quantum lift in their employment outcomes. In this way they could truly become part of mainstream Australia. Others were obsessed with re-adjudicating the past. To them it was all about guilt and dispossession.

Those different approaches largely continue. Most Australians then (as now) wanted to improve the lot of Aboriginal people; consistent with that, they valued the fact that they were part of Western civilisation, and knew that but for British settlement the modern, vibrant and free nation they loved and enjoyed would not have come about.

In the 18th century, colonisation of the Australian mainland by a European power was next to inevitable. The

British colonisation of Australia had many flaws, yet there is much in the assertion that the best thing that ever happened to Australia was to have been settled by the British.

We owe a lot to our British origins: the commonality of institutions, language, legal systems, press freedoms, sporting passions, in some respects our sense of humour, and so the list goes on. Yet we drew the line very early. Australians rejected class distinctions or any semblance of an aristocracy. These things were judged to be out of step with the distinctive society we had begun to build. Respect was never to morph into deference. Australia had chosen the good bits of our British inheritance, but rejected the bad bits, and the bits that were simply not fit for purpose.

This was an early illustration of what would grow to be one of the defining characteristics of our nation, and that was a sense of balance. I have chosen this phrase as the title of this volume, because it deals with topics in our current national discourse in which that sense of balance shines through.

The Hawke Government was in power when the bicentennial celebrations finally took place, and in an early act of cancel culture – an unknown expression in the 1980s – it discarded 'The Australian Achievement' in favour of the empty and limp tag of 'Living Together'. Not entirely clear about what the bicentenary should be celebrating, the government replaced a positive affirmation of what Australia had achieved in 200 years with a meaningless banality.

The major formal event of the 200th-anniversary party was at Sydney Cove on 26 January, addressed by the PM and Prince Charles. Right on song, it was interrupted by the arrival of the First Fleet re-enactment, which by then had become a private-enterprise venture. The government could no longer handle the sponsorship of what had begun as an official re-enactment of Phillip's epic First Fleet voyage that inaugurated modern Australia.

Some Aboriginal people objected to the bicentennial commemoration, consistent with their argument that Australia had been invaded. Wishing to accommodate Aboriginal opinion, and goaded by leftist apologists, who seemed ashamed of what Australia had become, the government separated itself from the re-enactment, secure in the knowledge that plenty of Australians, proud of what we had achieved, would pitch in to ensure that the expedition would not fail. But in a final act of hypocrisy, the official program for the day was arranged so that there was a gap to accommodate the arrival of the First Fleet re-enactment. Neither out of sight nor out of mind, but certainly out of official acknowledgement. Little was made of this at the time. Australians knew there was plenty about their country to celebrate.

Debate about 26 January as Australia Day continues. In this context it is worth noting that, in its historic *Mabo* judgement four years later, widely hailed as a landmark in achieving proper recognition of the First Australians, the

4

High Court of Australia did not question that Australia had been settled, as distinct from being either conquered or ceded. Mr Justice Toohey stated, inter alia: 'There is no question of annexation of the [Murray] Islands by conquest or cession, so it must be taken that they were acquired by settlement even though, long before European contact, they were occupied and cultivated by the Meriam people.'[1] Much of the basis of the court's conclusion that native title survived on the Murray Islands was that Australia had not been conquered but settled. Given that invasion normally precedes conquest this continues to present a dilemma for those who describe 26 January as 'Invasion Day'.[2]

During the years that I served in the national parliament I came to further understand the special character of our country; to appreciate its strengths and weaknesses; and most importantly to respect that sense of balance in the formulation of public policy that has long defined us as a people.

Nowhere is this more apparent than in the area of social-welfare provision, where Australia well and truly occupies the sweet spot. Our treatment of the genuinely disadvantaged both avoids the harshness of the American approach and eschews the paternalism adopted in many European countries, which discourages self-reliance and robs labour markets of the flexibility so important for economic efficiency.

One expression of this 'sweet spot' is found in how the government and private sectors interact with one another in relation to both health and education. A feature of Australia's very successful response to the COVID-19 pandemic has been the relatively seamless way in which the public and private elements of our health system have joined forces. It was starkly obvious from the beginning that the success of contact tracing would be crucial in the fight against COVID, so state public health authorities have masterminded on-the-ground responses. The relative success of New South Wales in this endeavour speaks volumes for the efficiency of its decentralised yet tightly coordinated health system. Private hospitals stood ready to provide additional care capacity when needed.

Vaccination has been carried out with like cooperation. GPs and pharmacists have provided the willing community backbone, augmented by mass vaccination hubs. Governments have controlled the procurement of vaccines and provided control and guidance as to priority groupings.

For several decades now, many of the old rivalries between public and private have been progressively dissolving. The Liberal and National Parties had once criticised Medicare, but finally embraced it before our victory at the 1996 election. Thenceforth the new health paradigm for the Coalition was to be Medicare appropriately strengthened over time, supported by an effective private hospital system.

The latter was to be sustained by a rebuilt private health insurance network, made possible by the blood transfusion of a generous non-means-tested tax incentive. The deal was that Medicare was to stay as the centre pole of the tent, and the old hostility towards private hospitals was to give way to an era of cooperation and, on occasions, colocation.

It would be idle to pretend that problems do not remain, but the clear collaboration between the two sectors during the pandemic revealed a new era of cooperation. Australians were no longer arguing so much about which was better, public or private. It was clear that we needed both.

The same approach is to be found within the education sector. Today approximately 34 per cent of Australian school-age children are educated at non-government schools; this compares with 10 per cent in the US, 8 per cent in Canada and 6 per cent in the UK.[3] These non-government schools range from the high-fee-paying private schools, such as the King's School in Sydney and Geelong College in Melbourne, to the low-fee-paying local Catholic parish schools. Pockets of resentment still exist against private schools, especially from those who will always object to taxpayer assistance of any kind ever going to parents of students attending non-government schools or to any of those schools themselves. Although the popular image of non-government schools is of the high-fee-paying kind, the real growth in the past 30 years has been in the low-fee-paying sector. That is where freedom of choice has broken through, because exercising that choice is affordable to a growing cohort of parents.

When, in 1956, I sat the Leaving Certificate from Canterbury Boys' High School, a selective high school within the New South Wales public system, the near-universal perception of the private school system (outside of the local Catholic parish schools) was that it was composed of the wealthy GPS schools such as King's, Scots and Riverview. More than 60 years on, the scene has been transformed. Now, as then, the wealthy GPS schools are still there, charging quite high fees, and within the reach of a small percentage of parents. They have been joined by a myriad of new independent schools, many of them Anglican, Christian (non-denominational) or Lutheran, and in some cases Jewish or Muslim. Typically, the fees charged would be in the range of $10,000 a year or less. This surge in more affordable private school options was a direct consequence of the removal by my government of a Hawke Government restriction denying federal funding to new independent schools in areas already serviced by a government and a Catholic school.

The Catholic parish-based system offers a parallel but separate narrative. When 'free, compulsory and secular' education was introduced in the 1860s, the Catholics elected to keep their own schools going. They were denied any government help, despite the fact that Catholic parents were to be found largely in the poorer sections of society. The Catholic system would eventually cater for about 20 per cent of the total school population, which took a huge financial burden off the state. The Catholic community was determined to maintain its own system, but it never tired of agitating for what became known as 'state aid'. It wanted government help to keep its system going.

That agitation lasted almost 100 years, but really acquired a head of steam in the 1950s, as the numbers of men and women entering Catholic teaching orders began to decline sharply. Having to employ increased numbers of lay teachers in response to a much smaller religious stream placed a huge additional financial burden on an already overstretched system. Appropriately enough, the issue was brought to a head through the inability of the local state schools to accommodate Catholic students in Goulburn in 1962. Those students had to leave their school because it could not afford to comply with a demand placed on it for a new toilet block by state health authorities. The Catholic authorities asked the government to pay for the new toilets, which the government refused to do. So, the Catholic students of Goulburn marched around the corner to the local state school and chaos ensued. The point was made.

Robert Menzies delivered the great breakthrough in 1963, with an election promise to provide extra money for science blocks in all schools – government and non-government – on an equal basis. This shift on state aid not only delivered justice to Australia's Catholic community, but it also did much to reduce sectarianism in our country.

In health, education and so many other areas we have achieved a middle way, a sensible compromise, an even-handed treatment of fiercely contested points of view. That sense of balance has contributed mightily to 'The Australian Achievement'.

There are many reasons behind it. There is a substantial deposit of Celtic scepticism within the population that has helped insulate Australians against extremist social, political and religious advocacy. It has not impeded deeply held commitments of conscience and faith, but there is often an inbuilt wariness in our response to the siren call of radical theories promising newly discovered solutions to age-old challenges. We are not a gullible people.

That we have been one of the world's longest functioning democracies, and have led the way in such areas as voting equality for women and the secret ballot, demonstrates a national self-confidence of which we should be more conscious. The absence of class barriers in Australia has stimulated a spirit of experimentation often constrained in more hierarchical societies.

The following series of reflections explores some of these issues.

As a person who has spent all his adult life involved in some manner in politics, it was impossible not to be aware of the near hysteria that emanated from sections of the political class when the British people voted to leave the European Union, and a few months later Donald Trump was elected US President. Meanwhile, Australia has earnt its own notoriety by cycling through no fewer than six prime ministers in just 11 years. Political parties across the world have seen increased factionalism and narrowing memberships. These developments have fuelled claims that democracy in Australia and elsewhere is under threat, with some polls recording a decline in support, especially among the young, for the proposition that democracy is the most desirable form of government. Political parties are no longer as representative as they once were of the sections of society disposed to support them, and I believe this has serious consequences for the effectiveness of political systems worldwide. I address this issue in the first three essays that follow. These issues are not peculiar to our country. They are to be found in other great democracies. I have attempted to address this issue especially in the context of the Brexit and Trump phenomena.

In the fourth essay, 'The Broad Church', I examine the balance between the classical liberal tradition and the conservative tradition that has characterised the Liberal Party of Australia since its founding. And, given that our nation now has historically high debt levels, in 'Bipartisanship:

A One-way Street', I have reflected on some past experiences in responding to both challenges and opportunities in the area of economic reform. The 25-year period encompassing the Hawke, Keating and Howard Governments saw a lot of economic reform, with plenty of bipartisanship, but only from the Coalition. Labor, in opposition after 1996, never returned the compliment. In doing that I recall a frequent observation of mine as PM that economic reform is akin to participating in a never-ending foot race. One knows that the finishing line will never be reached, but if you pull out or relax too much, your competitors will surge past you.

In other chapters I deal with issues such as constitutional change, the monarchy and what has happened over the 20 years since 9/11, as well as climate change, nuclear power and housing, which relate very much to the ongoing economic debate.

The past decade has seen a huge turnaround in Australian attitudes towards China. Handling this relationship is unquestionably our biggest foreign policy challenge at present. China is our largest export destination. Approximately 1.4 million Australians are of Chinese descent. Chinese is the most widely spoken foreign language in our country. It is appropriate that I turn to this relationship in the penultimate chapter.

There were unusual features of the recent federal election. The primary vote of the victorious Labor Party was by far the lowest of any victor in modern times. A new grouping – professing to be independents – captured six previously safely held Liberal seats. Debate has emerged as to how permanent these features will be. The final chapter contains my analysis of the election and offers some views of mine about the future direction of the Liberal Party.

Fundamental to the success of any political movement is to understand and constructively interpret the will of the electorate. It is appropriate, therefore, that I turn to an examination of the Brexit referendum and the election of Donald Trump as President of the United States.

THE MOB:
HOW DARE THEY!

Reflections on balancing the needs
of the party and the people

For students of politics, particularly in the Western world, 2016 was quite a year. Two events occurred that not only defied most predictions but also, according to many genuine as well as self-appointed experts, should never have happened. These were the British people's decision to leave the European Union (popularly known as Brexit), and the election of Donald Trump as President of the United States.

Although they were two entirely separate events, in two different if historically and politically close nations, it was convenient for commentators to lump them together. Both were branded as illustrations of unbridled and unacceptable populism. Without putting too fine a point on it, in both cases the mob had got it wrong. At least, that was the rather condescending view of the metropolitan elites.

There was at least one fundamental difference between the two events: Trump won in a regular presidential election, whereas Brexit triumphed in a once-in-a-lifetime referendum. Some of those who had opposed the split with the EU quickly sought refuge in the complicated withdrawal process as a way of frustrating the democratic decision of the British public. Before long they were calling for another referendum.

As someone who followed the campaigns in Britain and the United States closely, I was delighted with Britain's decision to leave the EU but had genuinely mixed feelings about Donald Trump's victory.

A presidential election always involves a binary choice. In that sense, Trump's win was barely surprising. It was his upset victory in the Republican primaries and his controversial style that gave his election particular moment. In addition, the rejection of Hillary Clinton, who would have been the first female president, was regarded by those who live and breathe identity politics as unforgivable.

When Clinton and Trump squared off against each other in 2016, I probably felt, as many did, that American voters were faced with an uninspiring choice. Most would have felt the same when contemplating a choice between Biden and Trump in 2020. In 2012 the choice had been between Barack Obama and Mitt Romney, and that contest had seemed of a higher order. Each had a compelling story to tell. Obama, a highly skilled presenter, had become America's first ever black president. Yet neither he nor indeed Romney relied so heavily on identity or envy politics. Romney had enjoyed a stellar business career, largely without the controversy that had attended Trump's corporate forays.

Biden's defeat of Trump, and the appalling unwillingness of the former President to accept the umpire's decision, ought to have produced a firm repudiation of Trumpism by the Republican Party. His consistent unwillingness to accept the election result cruelled the Republicans' prospects of winning at least one of two vacant Georgia Senate seats. The Democrats took both in the elections that followed the presidential poll of 2020. This cost the Republicans control of the Senate. Yet Trump retains the affections of a depressingly large number of Republicans.

Surely the question is not whether he will run again, but whether the Republican Party will endorse him again. It was dumbfounding to me, and I am sure to many others, that the party should have chosen him as its candidate in 2016. He lacked public grace, a huge deficiency for an American president, who is both head of state and head of government. He had little respect for his party organisation, despite the support it gave him during the presidential campaign.

Those seeking a presidential nomination will generally be a diverse group; all they will have in common is a desire to claim the crown. Some will be state governors or city mayors; others will point to business or professional achievements. In 2016, Trump heralded his business attainments, but his principal promotional tool was his status as a TV celebrity. It can be said with certainty that in no way had his suitability for the office of President been tested against a common set of criteria.

In the US the President is not a member of Congress, nor are his cabinet secretaries. There is no such thing as an opposition leader in the US. There are majority and minority leaders in each of the two houses of Congress, but their status, although important, is limited to that. Because presidential candidates are not chosen as leaders by the congressional members of their parties, they have no ongoing status if they lose. Donald Trump may be the best-known Republican at present, but he has no political position beyond being the immediate past president.

Ironically, the system suits him, because he clearly intends to run again, and no other Republican can match him in notoriety. The tortuous US primary system means that, until the next Republican convention on the eve of the 2024 presidential elections, there is no other Republican standard-bearer.

Given Trump's atrocious behaviour after losing the 2020 election, which has surely made him unfit to return to the White House, this is a perplexing outcome. The party is consumed by pro- and anti-Trumpism. The ex-President looms as an ever-present reminder of a decision that cannot be made for over two years. If the Republicans choose to shun Trump in the future – as I certainly hope they will – then the operation of the American system gravely weakens their capacity to build an alternative narrative. By default, the former President just fills the space.

This has paralysed the party at a time when victory in the November 2022 mid-term elections appears likely. The incumbent President, Joe Biden, has had a very poor 18 months. His approval ratings are low, he displays regular evidence at news conferences of the beginnings of cognitive decline, and there is a mounting belief that he will not be re-endorsed as the Democratic Party candidate for the 2024 election. The Republican Party's electoral position could be greatly strengthened if it were able to choose its presidential candidate (if, of course, it is not Donald Trump) as soon as possible. The American electoral system denies it this opportunity.

The contrast with elections within a parliamentary system such as Australia's is stark. A Westminster system all but precludes the emergence of a 'wild card' candidate like Trump. Those seeking the leadership of the party are members of a small group. At a national level in Australia, this group usually numbers fewer than 100. They all know each other well, since they work together as MPs.

Potential candidates must be elected to parliament and run the gauntlet of microscopic examination by parliamentary colleagues before having a hope of winning the party leadership. Through that process, the relative abilities of aspirants are measured, weaknesses emerge and personality flaws become apparent. Then and only then does the glittering prize of the prime ministership appear within reach.

To my mind, the current status of Donald Trump illustrates another of the strengths of the parliamentary system. In Australia, a defeated PM either remains in the ring as opposition leader or is replaced by a new leader. There is no vacuum. When I lost the 2007 federal election, and my own seat, the Liberal Party chose Brendan Nelson as its new leader, and he became leader of the opposition. In concert with his senior colleagues, he set about recasting the alternative government of the country and preparing for the next election. He had the authority and responsibility to speak for the opposition on all issues.

The relative merits of the presidential and parliamentary systems are, nonetheless, largely academic. Neither is about to be replaced by the other, in either the United States or nations with parliamentary governments such as Australia.

The challenge here is to understand how effectively both of the two systems have responded to some of their recent challenges. The spectre of Trump has virtually paralysed the US Republican Party since his defeat in 2020. And in

Britain, which operates under a parliamentary system like Australia's, the Brexit phenomenon has had a similar impact. Prime Minister David Cameron, having campaigned for Britain to stay in Europe, felt obliged to resign when the decision went the other way. The Conservative Party then went through years of instability that has not yet abated.

The British people were happy with David Cameron and his Conservative government at the time of the Brexit referendum. He led the first Conservative government for 20 years and enjoyed a comfortable majority. Equally, though, a clear majority of Conservative voters wanted their nation to leave the European Union.

This issue had divided not only the Conservative Party but the whole of the British public for decades. Attitudes to Europe had figured prominently in leadership disputes in the ruling party, especially when Margaret Thatcher was removed as leader and PM. Arguments over Europe featured regularly during John Major's time in power.

Although there had been a confirmatory referendum in June 1975 in favour of the decision to join Europe, the British people had since lived through decades of trimmed sovereignty and the ever-growing centralised bureaucracy of the European behemoth. They had also watched a European world reach that fell well short of the 'third force' promised by Prime Minister Edward Heath and others when Britain joined the European Economic Community in 1973. For example, it was still the United States, through the agency of NATO, that had forced the settlement so desperately needed to end the chaos and bloodshed that followed the disintegration of the former Yugoslavia in the 1980s. The United States was seen to have filled the gap left by European nations.

To many Britons, the experience of being part of Europe had been poor recompense for what they regarded as turning their backs on the 'old Commonwealth' that included Canada, Australia and New Zealand. By 2016, many had begun to realise that the future of the world was at least as dependent on what happened in the Indo-Pacific as it was on European affairs. By dint of language, culture and history, the United Kingdom could better understand that part of the world than could many other nations.

Then, most importantly, there was migration. The United Kingdom is a small, crowded nation. The surge of asylum seekers from many sources, including the Middle East, had since the early 2000s created the perception that Europe and therefore Britain was being swamped with new arrivals. Strong migration from countries such as Poland and other former Soviet Bloc nations that had joined the EU in the early 2000s had had a significant impact on Britain's domestic labour market.

Free movement of labour was a key European Union protocol. Its benefits were appreciated when unmet need was accommodated; its potential menace emerged when locals lost their jobs to hard-working new residents. Those who argued for Britain to leave Europe could assert with some force that their country no longer controlled its borders. As someone who declared in 2001 that 'We will decide who comes to this country and the circumstances in which they come', I understood the force of that argument. 'Take back control' became a powerful Leave mantra during the Brexit referendum.

Far too many Remainers mistakenly believed that the nation state had entered its twilight period. To them, the concept of European citizenship – as distinct from or even opposed to, say, British, French or German citizenship – had real appeal. This was particularly the case in the Greater London area, where some 64 per cent would vote to remain.

I have long thought that the nation state remains the key organising principle for the conduct of international relations, notwithstanding the importance of bodies such as the United Nations. In 2015, I wrote an article for the *National Review* entitled 'Long Live the Nation-state', citing long-standing Singapore PM Lee Kuan Yew as an exemplar of outstanding leadership of a distinctive nation state.[1] No one has come near Lee in demonstrating how successful a well-led nation state can become, despite, in Singapore's case, such an inauspicious start. In that same *National Review* piece, I cast doubt on the then widespread prediction that Britain would vote to remain, highlighting the ongoing importance of the nation state as a factor that would work in the opposite direction.

It had been a Conservative campaign promise prior to the 2015 election to hold a Brexit referendum. Nick Clegg, Liberal Democrat leader and Deputy PM in Cameron's coalition government between 2010 and 2015, bitterly attacked Cameron over holding the referendum in the first place. He was a dedicated European, unquestionably sore about the rout of his party in the 2015 general election and argued that Cameron had used the referendum to solve an internal Conservative Party argument. George Osborne, Chancellor of the Exchequer and a close friend of Cameron, argued against holding the referendum but went along with his leader.

More than many at the top of his party, Cameron sensed the latent hostility of the British electorate towards Europe and knew there had to be a referendum giving voters a binary choice, but he underestimated just how strong the anti-European sentiment really was.

Why didn't Cameron press for a better deal out of Brussels, with the threat that he would campaign to leave if he did not get it? In the prelude to the referendum, Cameron traipsed around European capitals seeking concessions from his then EU colleagues. I was astonished at how little he wrung from them. I recall watching the news conference in

February 2016 at which he announced the new understanding that was to form the basis of his plea for Britain to stay with Brussels. The strongest argument that emerged was that the UK would never adopt the Euro. There was nothing new about that. It had been resolved years earlier when Tony Blair was in power. It was never again seriously in dispute. The concession Cameron extracted over migration was too heavily caveated to cut through to the British electorate.

Cameron presumed that his authority and that of Chancellor George Osborne would carry the day. He had just won an election in his own right, against expectations. There was an air of 'We know best' about the Conservative leadership on Europe.

Among other blunders, the Remain campaign exaggerated the economic consequences of Britain's departure from the EU. The Treasury and even the Bank of England abandoned impartiality as the vote neared. The strident campaign against Brexit was rightly dubbed 'Project Fear', and predictions of emergency budgets and drastic fiscal tightening if the UK voted Leave betrayed the sense of panic that had begun to grip the formerly over-confident Remain camp. Barack Obama's announcement that Britain would be at the end of the queue in negotiating a free trade pact with the US if it voted to leave was a huge tactical error. It was resented by the British public and reflected badly on Cameron's judgement. It is inconceivable that the

US President would have made that comment on his own initiative.

Before the 2015 election, I had discussed Brexit with Theresa May, then Home Secretary in the coalition government, at a London dinner party. She said that the Conservatives had to focus on the economy in order to win the imminent contest. She was right, but what surprised me was her marked reluctance to engage with the EU question.

Electorally, the economy was paramount in the immediate future, but membership of the European Union was a live issue that could not be wished away. Many British people had deep feelings about it, and had had them for a long time. This was especially the case for many traditional conservatives. Euroscepticism was widespread among the Conservative rank and file, yet there was an attitude of 'They have nowhere else to go' towards these supporters among many in the Conservative hierarchy.

Given the opportunity of an in-or-out referendum, they certainly *found* somewhere to go. In similar vein was the response of some in the Liberal Party of Australia who took for granted the loyalty of certain of their supporters on issues at the last election. I deal with this in the concluding chapter of the book.

One conclusion to be drawn from the Leave campaign was that misapplying the lessons of history can be as bad as ignoring them. It has long been a powerful argument that enduring cooperation between France and Germany, especially within a family of European nations, would spare the world from the horrors of the two wars that had cost millions of lives in the previous century. While all could agree on that, realising such a goal did not require each European nation to surrender ever-increasing amounts of national independence.

Nothing, however, could gainsay the dominance of migration as an issue. The main problem the Remain camp had was that it was seen, fairly or unfairly, as supporting continued high levels of immigration from Europe. The Conservative leadership was strongly arguing to stay in the EU. The Labour leadership did not bring much energy to the campaign, but the public remembered that it was during the Tony Blair–Gordon Brown years that large-scale Eastern European migration commenced.

Only Nigel Farage and his United Kingdom Independence Party were clearly seen as being against large-scale immigration. Though branded as an extremist by many, including high-ranking Conservatives, Farage had a big impact on the campaign. His message was clear and consistent. His views often echoed those of ordinary Britons. When, on the morning after the vote, with the lead of the Leave campaign appearing unassailable, Farage said, 'This is a victory for real people, for ordinary people, for decent people,' he undoubtedly expressed the sentiments of millions who felt that for too long their views had been treated with contempt and condescension by the political establishment.

Five years on, Boris Johnson, in so many ways a colourful and effective communicator and unquestionably the driving force behind the victorious Brexit campaign, is now in a world of woe with the British public and his own party. For a man of immense intelligence, he has failed to understand the feelings of those ordinary people who voted so strongly for him just two and a half years ago. Were he and his close coterie of advisors so out of touch that they imagined they could hold parties in Downing Street, when, according to the rules they had imposed, parties were banned for the ordinary person in their homes or workplaces? It seems obvious that the average British voter, burdened with the restrictions flowing from the pandemic and, in isolated cases, denied compassionate contact with close family members or friends, would react very badly to a clear double standard in behaviour from the Prime Minister and those immediately around him.

Aggrieved Remainers rounded on David Cameron for calling the referendum in the first place. He could scarcely escape criticism over his conduct of the campaign, or the reform deal he had negotiated with the Europeans, but to attack him for having given the British public the democratic right to decide the issue revealed the cynicism of his critics. If the result had gone the other way, those self-same critics would have acclaimed Cameron as a hero, and of course a true democrat.

Following the referendum, journalist David Goodhart wrote *The Road to Somewhere*, in which he substantially divided Britain into the 'Somewheres' and the 'Anywheres'.[2] The former group, often poorer and less well educated, felt a strong attachment to a local community, and by extension to their nation. The latter group were socially liberal and largely university-educated, and many saw themselves as citizens of the world. The analysis suggested that the Somewheres mostly voted Leave and the Anywheres Remain. Although Goodhart's book contained exaggerations, it was a perceptive take on the mood of Britain in the early part of this century. Importantly, it offered a social explanation of the outcome of the referendum.

The common response in circumstances such as the fallout from Brexit and the Trump election is to blame 'the system' – to find fault with the electoral process or, more outrageously, to blame the politicians for asking the people their opinion, as occurred in Britain. The parliamentary and presidential electoral systems both have their flaws. Yet despite Donald Trump's fulminations, elections in countries such as Britain, Australia and the US are clean. Electoral boundaries in Australia are more fairly drawn than in the US. Australia's preferential voting system results in more representative outcomes than Britain's first-past-the-post approach. Yet these are questions of degree and are subject to fierce debate.

Both the 2016 election and referendum results produced a mountain of commentary that called into question the workings of the democratic process. Not a little of it contained an element of intellectual snobbery. The people to blame were those less well educated Americans who had voted for Trump, and the British workers who felt threatened by Eastern European migrants who were supposedly after their jobs. It was certainly the case that Trump had attracted a strong vote in the de-industrialised Midwest, and that many British workers, particularly in the North of England, worried about the high rate of migration that membership of the European Union had produced.

Not only was there more to it than that, but both of those groups in the two countries also had legitimate reasons to feel insecure. It was a natural part of the political process for them to give expression to their concerns when they voted.

Instead of focusing on the bad judgement of those who voted allegedly out of unsophisticated populism, perhaps commentators should have turned their attention to the composition and functioning of political parties today? Perhaps it was the *parties*, not the *voters*, who got it wrong? Political parties have never been as representative of the different strains of public opinion as they might imagine, but is that more so the case now than ever before?

While two events in Britain and the United States respectively are the inspiration, if I may put it that way, for the examination of Australian political parties that I conduct in the next two chapters, the observations I make have relevance to most democratic nations.

Instead of blaming the system why don't we see if fault lies with those who *operate* the system, that is, the political parties? The basic elements of the political systems of Australia, the United Kingdom and the United States have not changed very much since, say, Ben Chifley succeeded the deceased John Curtin as PM of Australia, Winston Churchill attended his last 'Big Three' conference in Potsdam, and Franklin Delano Roosevelt was elected US President for a fourth term. All three events occurred in 1945.

Yet what *has* changed is the nature and composition of the major political parties of those three nations in the almost 80 years since then. That extended period embraced Margaret Thatcher's lengthy and reformist term and her partnership with Ronald Reagan, which saw the end of the old Soviet Union. In Australia it embraced the remarkable 16 years in power of Robert Menzies, Australia's longest serving PM. It also produced Bob Hawke, seen by many as our nation's best Labor PM.

For Australians, it is almost a badge of honour to be cynical about the operation of our political system. Yet beyond a near-obsession with personal rivalries within our political parties, most of us spend little time analysing the pathologies of those parties, and the vastly different environment in which they have now operated for some years.

Neither the Liberal nor the Labor Party was ever a mass movement in the proper sense of that term, although the ALP for a time went closer, largely because of its trade union roots. It is undeniable, though, that over the past 30 to 40 years political party memberships have not only declined numerically, but also ceased to be as broadly representative of distinct strains of political and economic opinion in the community, committed to achieving certain policy goals, as once was the case.

Historically, for example, many people joined the ALP to achieve fairer wealth distribution, and the Liberal Party recruited members who wanted to defend private enterprise against government interference. Although these and other broad goals still motivate many party members, both parties increasingly include groups of men and women consumed by single issues and the modern phenomenon of identity politics. Factionalism is on the rise. Parties are beset by internal rivalries and no longer united by anything other than a thirst for office.

When I first became active in politics in the early 1960s, what I described as the 40–40–20 rule obtained. This meant that 40 per cent always voted for the ALP, 40 per cent for the Coalition, and 20 per cent floated between the two, or voted for minor parties or independents. In recent years I have commonly remarked that perhaps the old 40–40–20 rule has been replaced by a 30–30–40 rule.

The reality, however, is that although both major parties have shed votes to minor parties and independents, Australia remains firmly with the two-party paradigm, despite predictions after bad results that one or other of them faced an existential crisis. The May 2022 poll did return Labor to power after nine years in opposition, although its primary vote of just under one-third of the electorate underscored the almost grudging nature of its victory. The unexpected strength of the so-called teal vote in former Liberal strongholds should have served notice on both the Liberal and Labor Parties that no section of the electorate can ever be taken for granted.

It should also be kept in mind that sustained support for one of the major parties at a federal level is often balanced by long periods of government by the other side at a state level. The situation prior to May of this year is a case in point. The Federal Coalition had been in power for 19 of the previous 25 years. Yet for most of that time, the ALP governed Victoria and Queensland. The last state election in Western Australia reduced the Liberal Party to a rump of only two seats in the lower house. After only four years of Liberal government, South Australia early in 2022 re-elected a Labor government. For most of the almost 12 years that the Howard Government was in office, Labor was usually in power at a state level. It governed New South Wales, the largest state, for the entirety of my administration. There has never been such a thing as a natural party of government in Australia.

As I discuss in my next chapter, 'Bowling Alone', there is a growing cohort in both our major parties whose whole working life has been spent in and around politics. Many of these people regard themselves as being involved in the political game, not in the pursuit of a better society. And, as I argue in 'Choosing the Leader', disposable party leaders have become a by-product of this new mindset.

A recent European study claimed that 'the proportion of believers is likely to shrink while the proportion of careerists is likely to grow ... As a result, politics has become more and more about the competition between professionalised party elites and less about the mobilisation and integration of socially distinct groups'[3] This is borne out by the behaviour of political parties in relation to both the Trump election and the Brexit referendum.

Both events raise fundamental questions about the nature of political parties in today's environment. Why, after dominating the scene in two of the world's most durable democracies, have major political parties in both the US and the UK recently produced such uninspiring flag-carriers, and proven so unable to understand the mood of their electorates? Is there something so wrong with the way in which Western political parties now function that some of the leaders they produce prove unable to match the great political moments they face? Have their memberships become so narrow that they no longer truly understand what the public wants and believes in? Even more to the point, have they become too obsessed with internal issues and lost sight of their fundamental mission, which is to effectively reflect the views of the community, and not just narrow sections of it?

Intense analysis of the May election in Australia, especially the strong performance of the teal candidates, is required. As already accepted, that performance sent a clear message to the major parties that no section of the electorate can ever be taken for granted. In many ways the teal performance was evidence that many voters had grown weary with the internal preoccupations of political parties and their lack of clearly communicated convictions, and they reacted accordingly. Lest those elected as independents in seats such as Kooyong in Melbourne and North Sydney see a new dawn, they should understand that the mood that swept them in can easily take them away, and as early as the next election.

BOWLING ALONE

Reflections on the need for balance within the membership of political parties

In 2000, Robert Putnam published the book *Bowling Alone*, which analysed the decline in the US over the previous half-century in participation in associations and societal groups.[1] More broadly, he traced the decline in what has come to be called social capital – that is, the value to society when individuals band together for a common cause or purpose. Such meetings are not only valuable for that purpose, but also for the satisfaction and happiness derived by those who have come together. And, it might be added, for the proper functioning of democracy.

The book's title was drawn from one of the remarkable discoveries Putnam made: that there had been a sharp increase in the number of Americans who literally went to bowling alleys to play on their own. Historically, bowling had been a pastime enjoyed by groups, a widely employed opportunity for socialising. This change was a vivid metaphor for the wider conclusions he had reached.

Putnam argued that those born in the 1920s and 1930s were the last of the 'joiners', as demonstrated by higher levels of civic participation across the board by people of that generation. The evidence he assembled suggested that Americans who came of age during the Depression and World War II were more deeply involved in the life of their communities than the generations that followed.

Having examined all possible contributors to this great change, Putnam concluded that the proliferation of television from 1950 onwards provided the major explanation. As he wrote in 1996 in *Prospect* magazine, barely 10 per cent of US homes had TV sets in 1950, but by 1959 – in what he described as probably the fastest diffusion of a technological innovation ever recorded – they could be found in 90 per cent of American households.[2]

The decade of the 1950s has long been seen in the US as a period of almost idyllic middle-class stability and optimism. The country had recovered from the war, wages and employment were rising, housing was plentiful, the baby boomer generation was in full swing, and society was yet to be touched by the social upheaval of the 1960s and the deep divisions engendered by the Vietnam War. In my view, though, the social revolutionary mood of the 1960s was itself another factor that contributed to the participation decline, involving as it did the rejection of so many of the practices and attitudes of the prevailing culture. Inevitably, this meant that because Mum and Dad had joined a particular group, their offspring would not. Increasingly people stopped joining.

The huge increase in female workforce participation is another major cause. It has greatly changed one of the old models, whereby Dad came home from work, ate the meal that Mum had prepared for him, then went off to the latest meeting of his party or union or other group. That may sound like an over-simplification, but the surge of women into the workforce from the 1970s has wrought permanent changes to the way we function as communities. The failure of many organisations, including political parties, to fully adjust to this change has in some cases been just as responsible for the membership erosion as the change itself.

In so many ways, Putnam's observations find an echo in Australia. Our society too has produced an intricate network of local groups, commonly built around school, sporting, church and other activities. An added accelerant of this in both the US and Australia has been the relative absence of a class structure, which has removed a potential impediment to meeting together (though in the US particularly, racial differences have sometimes acted as a further brake).

Putnam traced the decline in the membership of a variety of organisations. The trends would have been largely duplicated in Australia, although the starting points would have varied. Church affiliations have been stronger for longer among Americans, but trade union memberships reached higher levels in Australia than they ever did in the US.

The trade union movement has also seen the most dramatic decline in participation of Australians. When I entered parliament in 1974, union membership was a little over 48 per cent. By 2020 it had fallen to just 14.3 per cent. At present there are more female than male members of unions. Education and training has become the most highly unionised cohort, followed by public administration and safety, then healthcare and social caring.[3] The traditional image of a unionist as a hard-working manufacturer or miner, usually covered in grit and almost always male, is no longer remotely accurate. This process was aided by my government's passage of the *Workplace Relations Act* in 1996, which prohibited compulsory unionism and the closed shop.

Very few organisations have escaped the decline. Churches and church-affiliated groups, service clubs such as Rotary, and even local Parents & Citizens and Parents & Friends associations have been affected. It has likewise been the case with many local sporting groups.

When *Bowling Alone* was published, the full impact of the internet, mobile phones and other information technology had yet to be experienced. The hand-held device has delivered immense independence and security. Yet it has come at the cost of markedly reducing or even eliminating physical contact in groups. At the most basic level, why do the four of us need to meet for morning coffee if we can just catch up on Facebook? As Putnam's book made clear, declining and narrowing membership was a problem long before the explosion of social media and information technology. The latter have not only reinforced the effect of television in individualising our existences, but have taken them to a new dimension.

Carried forward, this has huge implications for the operation of groups such as political parties, which thrive on direct personal discourse and the lively exchange of ideas. As I asserted in the previous chapter, parties across the board have become smaller and less representative of their constituents. Growing individualism is just one of many reasons for this. Other changes in society's structures and behaviour have contributed; so have cultural changes peculiar to each party.

For instance, it may seem strange to say so now, but the Cold War and the decades-long ideological struggle between the capitalist West and the Soviet-led East, whose rival economic ethos was driven by high levels of state control, provided something of the background noise to the battle between the major political forces not only in Australia, but around the world. It was particularly relevant to the factional contests within the Labor Party.

Factionalism has been a constant in politics – in Australia and worldwide – but, as I shall argue, over the past three or four decades factionalism has taken on a new complexion.

In the past 100 years the ALP has had three major splits. The first was over conscription for military service in World War I. The next surrounded the appropriate economic response to the Great Depression. The third was over the influence of communism within the ALP. This last one provoked the great ALP schism of the 1950s, which denied Labor any chance of national office for more than a generation.

For at least 20 years, the party tore itself apart over how much of the socialist economic philosophy it should embrace, and how closely Australia should align itself with the United States in the Cold War. Similar struggles befell some other centre-left parties around the world. In Australia the convulsion contained the added component of sectarianism, and a new party, the Democratic Labour Party (DLP), emerged. As late as 1969, the preferences of the DLP played a crucial role in the re-election of the Coalition.

Whitlam's 1972 victory provided deliverance for the party from two decades of opposition and intense factionalism. Ironically, though, this was the era in which factionalism began to change from a contest of ideas into an empty political game.

By then, the patent decline of the Eastern Bloc as any kind of plausible rival to the capitalist West meant that the prize fighters had been left without a ring in which to box. The ideological issues might have dissolved, but the factions were still there. Many, however, had no idea what was left to argue about, except personal preferment within the party. (That is, until the rise more than three decades later of identity politics and climate change as major political battlegrounds.)

The Liberal Party, meanwhile, featured little factionalism from its inception in the 1940s until the Whitlam years. Much of this was due to the dominance of Menzies over the party, and the resultant national political hegemony that lasted for almost a quarter of a century. There was no serious questioning of economic direction, and Liberals united behind the foreign policy stances of their pro-American, Anglophile PM. Seven successive electoral victories suggested he must have got something right. Even after Menzies left the stage, factionalism did not emerge for some years, and then in a stuttering fashion.

Sadly, it was mainly built around personalities and preferment, rather than policy differences. When I entered parliament in 1974, I was immediately conscious of division in the ranks of Liberal senators and MPs from Victoria. It was not based on policy or ideology but derived from the stances different people had taken when John Gorton was removed from the leadership three years before. As I explain in the next chapter, 'Choosing the Leader', major policy differences lay behind Gorton's downfall, but from it emerged increasingly bitter personal and factional disputes. There was an identifiable group, which included some beyond Victoria, whose main organising principle was to stop Malcolm Fraser from ever becoming leader. He was blamed for Gorton's downfall as PM.

Fraser's massive win at the 1975 election submerged any nascent factionalism in the party. It was not until three elections later, and back in opposition, that some factionalism resurfaced. It took the form of differences over economic policy (which I shall discuss in 'Bipartisanship: A One-way Street'), coupled with competing leadership ambitions (as canvassed in the next chapter). As a result, the Liberal Party of the mid-1980s was a noticeably different one from that inherited from Bob Menzies by Harold Holt 20 years earlier.

Factionalism alone did not account for this difference. The membership of political parties was also becoming less diverse, and this phenomenon too had its origins in the era of tumultuous change following Whitlam's defeat of the long-standing Liberal government.

When I first became an MP, I was entitled to just one staff member, an electorate secretary, who obviously needed advanced office skills and high-grade stenographic talents.

Almost always female, these staffers held the fort in electorate offices during MPs' frequent absences in Canberra and were invaluable in dealing with constituents' issues. There was also a small typing pool in Canberra to assist with anything urgent while parliament was sitting.

When the Whitlam Government was returned at the 1974 election with a reduced majority, it became critically dependent on a small number of very marginal seats. In early 1975, Fred Daly, the minister in charge of parliamentary staff matters, announced that henceforth every member and senator in the parliament would be entitled to an additional staffer. That person could be assigned any duties the MP or senator deemed relevant to his or her work.

The political motives were obvious. On one occasion at Sydney Airport, Liberal senator John Carrick and I ran into Daly, an immensely likeable character who had forgotten more about the dark political arts than most people accumulated in a lifetime. John said to him: 'Freddie, I see you've given all your marginal seat holders a field officer.' Without blushing, Daly mumbled something about massively increased workloads.

Carrick had nailed it. This extra staff person would be devoted to shoring up the electoral position of individual Labor MPs in narrowly held seats. At the time there was less pressure on occupants of marginal Coalition seats, but that would ebb and flow according to the political climate.

So was born the era of the political staffer. This decision by Daly created a whole new career path and would, over time, have a profound impact on the workings of parliament house, intensify factionalism, especially in the Liberal Party, and progressively alter the broad composition of parliamentary ranks. These developments would be reflected at a state level, as state governments readily followed their federal peers.

Until then there had been very few staff positions for those who wanted a full-time job in or around politics. Most ministerial staffers came from public service departments; there were a very small number of positions within state divisions of the Liberal Party, or the party's Federal Secretariat. If you were a political activist, you did politics at night or during weekends.

Over time, though, MP staff positions would grow to four for each member. Many extremely dedicated and capable young men and women would join the staff of MPs, but nothing could gainsay the fact that a huge cultural change was under way. An ambitious person could go to university, join a union office (in the case of Labor members), obtain a staff position, then seek preselection for a seat. To many would-be politicians, it was a dream path come true.

Two former staffers of mine, Anthony Roberts and David Elliott, became respectively the Minister for Homes and Minister for Planning, and the Minister for Transport and Minister for Veterans in the current New South Wales government. Each did an excellent job for me, and they are fine ministers in that government. Both, incidentally, served in the Army Reserve, with Elliott doing a tour of duty in Bougainville. Another of my former staffers, Tim James, won the state seat of Willoughby for the Liberal Party early in 2022, following the resignation of Gladys Berejiklian as New South Wales Premier.

It is important here to separate out people whose pre-parliamentary careers have included a staff period that could in no way be regarded as having defined their career path. Former Liberal senator Arthur Sinodinos, now Australia's ambassador to the United States, was my outstanding chief of staff for 10 years, and before that held other positions on my staff. Yet he was a highly skilled economist, who came to my employ from the Treasury. He left a senior position in that department to rejoin my staff after I became opposition leader again early in 1995. But for his economic background I would not have employed him in the first place.

Josh Frydenberg, who did an admirable job as Treasurer before his defeat in the May election, does not easily fit any description. He was a senior advisor of mine when I was PM. Before that he had held a like role with Alexander Downer. Joshua left my office in 2005 to take up a position with Deutsche Bank, where he worked until entering parliament at the 2010 election.

It is very much in the public interest that the parliaments of the Commonwealth and states be composed of a wide cross-section of people, so that those who make decisions have some understanding from their own life experiences of the difficulties that confront their fellow citizens in their daily lives. There can never be one occupation that prepares an MP for this task. The best one can hope for is that there will always be a wide variety of occupational backgrounds among state and federal politicians, so that governmental decisions are as fully informed as they can be.

It is a paradox that at a time when trade union membership is demonstrably lower than decades ago, the number of ALP MPs who were formerly trade union officials remains disproportionately high.

Random comparisons can be both dangerous and revealing. The Chifley Labor cabinet that lost to Menzies in 1949 was composed of a much wider spread of occupational backgrounds than that of the Rudd Labor cabinet that lost to Tony Abbott in 2013. That Chifley cabinet included one lawyer, four farmers, a dentist, a publican and a tobacconist (now that almost brands you a criminal!). Its only lawyer, H.V. Evatt, had been a High Court judge. The Rudd cabinet contained no one with a rural background, and only Joel Fitzgibbon could claim even a tenuous connection with small business. Seven of Kevin Rudd's team had been party officials or political staffers. Five had been trade union officials.

The passage of time has not altered much for the Labor Party. The Albanese cabinet is dominated by former trade union officials and political staffers. Only Mark Dreyfus, the Attorney-General, worked unambiguously in the private sector for an extended period. He became a QC in 1999. Several worked as lawyers in private practice or government departments. None appears to have been involved in small business. Chifley's cabinet, dare I say it, was a model of diversity.

In the years of the Fraser Government, the influence of farmers in the cabinet was often criticised – in my view without reason. In that cabinet there were six farmers, and none were of the Pitt or Collins Street variety. There were also three lawyers contributing to a total cabinet of then just 12. Twenty years later, the first Howard cabinet included four farmers and seven lawyers out of a cabinet total of 14.

Remarkably, the previous parliament included only four members who identified as farmers, graziers or primary producers: three Liberals and one National. That is a far cry from earlier years, and most significantly reveals a much-changed National Party. Given what our nation owes to rural Australia, this should give us pause to reflect.

Some years ago, there was a frequent refrain that there were 'too many lawyers in parliament'. This complaint is rarely heard today because it is no longer true. Some have suggested that the cry these days, especially at a state level, should be that there are 'too many staffers'. Nine of the 23 members of the first Morrison cabinet had worked as staffers. Thirteen of the 24 members of the last Berejiklian cabinet in New South Wales had worked as staffers.

It is all a question of degree. MPs who have been staffers bring with them into parliament skills and knowledge that it can take others a long time to acquire. Some never do. My concern is that political parties are selecting representatives from a narrowing group of men and women whose entire working life experience has been within the mechanics of politics. The cold statistics suggest this. Within the parliament elected in 2016, 49 per cent of Liberal MPs had previously worked in state or federal politics – as staffers, party officials or corporate affairs employees of companies largely involved in political liaison.

This has the potential to become a self-reinforcing process. The natural shrinkage of membership increases the power of factions, which lack the motivation to recruit new members through fear of upsetting factional balances.

Most of the staffers recruited over the years have worked diligently in their jobs and contributed to the overall cause, but unavoidably they have become part of these growing factional divisions. Those working for senators and for MPs in safe seats have had ample time for internal party affairs and, dare I say it, such things as branch stacking. Networking between staffers has reinforced the factional divisions.

Not only are Liberal MPs labelled as either small-l Liberals or conservatives or moderates or whatever, but so are staff.

The most negative consequence of factionalism is that political parties have become more inward-looking, less welcoming to newcomers. They are increasingly preoccupied with themselves, to the detriment of engaging with and understanding the thinking of the community.

Ridiculous manifestations of factionalism within the Liberal Party have included the so-called 'Black Hand' dinners, held in conjunction with the annual Federal Council gathering. I am told they are composed of the small-Liberals and their sympathisers. I can't be certain, because I have never attended one. I *can* be certain there is a rival dinner, because I was invited to address the one held in conjunction with the Sydney Federal Council meeting in 2018. I declined the invitation because I had no desire to give further currency to factional divisions.

The greatest cultural change of the past few decades has been in the attitude towards what was once called branch development. Previously, the main pursuit of a lively branch was to build membership. These days building membership has given way to adopting strategies to stop the branch from being 'taken over' by a rival faction. New members are viewed suspiciously, lest they upset the factional balance.

My knowledge of the New South Wales Division is more extensive than of other divisions, but intense factional struggles persist in other states too. The appalling performance of the West Australian Liberals at the recent state election exemplified the working out of factional rivalry. That division had been hollowed out by factional warfare, and the disastrous consequences were there for all to see. And while I don't put it in the same category as the West Australian Division, factional rifts during the Marshall Government's term of office in South Australia clearly played a role in its loss to the ALP in March 2022.

The decision of the New South Wales Division to endorse candidates for some local government elections was misguided. Local issues cut across normal party-political lines, and local government elections devour precious party resources, can sometimes involve branches in property development wrangles, and often attract interest from people who have little concern about the overall wellbeing of the Liberal Party. Perhaps the idea of endorsing local government candidates has taken hold because it provides the factions with more preselection goodies to hand around to the faithful. It makes sense for the Liberal Party to run candidates for the Brisbane City Council because, unlike other capital-city councils, it has state-government-like functions in some areas. That is a rarity.

In case my judgements seem harsh, let's apply a test that should be widely accepted by all Liberals, and that is the test of the market. Forty to fifty years ago, preselection contests in Liberal-held seats attracted much larger fields of candidates. In mid-1973, the former Foreign Minister in the McMahon Government, Nigel Bowen, was appointed to the New South Wales Court of Appeal. A by-election in his seat of Parramatta became necessary. It was anything but a safe seat: Bowen had held it by just a few hundred votes at the 1972 election. Despite this, no fewer than 30 people sought preselection. Philip Ruddock won the contest, and would become the second longest serving MP, after Billy Hughes, in the history of the federal parliament. One of the excellent candidates he defeated was the late Nick Shehadie, a former Wallabies captain, who later became Lord Mayor of Sydney and Chairman of SBS.

Just 18 months earlier Tom Hughes, Attorney-General in the Gorton Government, had signalled his retirement at the 1972 election, throwing open his seat of Berowra which was comprised of staunchly Liberal areas. The preselection attracted 33 aspirants. I was one of the unsuccessful 32. Dr Harry Edwards, a Berowra local and Professor of Economics at Macquarie University, took it out. It was a strong field which also included a gifted physician, Peter Baume, later a senator; Jim Cameron, a local state MLA; and other prominent figures in the party organisation. Also of real note was Bob Ellicott, then Solicitor-General of the Commonwealth, later MP for Wentworth and Attorney-General in the Fraser Government.

Then in late 1973 three safe seats – Wentworth, and the adjoining seats of Bradfield and Bennelong – brought forth competitive preselections. In Bradfield and Bennelong, long-standing MPs were retiring, and in Wentworth, the former Treasurer and Foreign Minister Leslie Bury was under real threat. The three preselections took place within days of each other. David Connolly, a diplomat, won Bradfield from a field of 29, I was successful in Bennelong against 24 other contestants, and Bob Ellicott defeated Bury against 15 others.

More than 30 years later, Alan Cadman, who had entered parliament with me in 1974, was under real pressure to call it a day in Mitchell, covering the Hills district of Sydney. He was challenged by what could only be called a small and modest field. This was surprising, as Mitchell was about as blue a seat as one could find, having a margin of close to 20 per cent. It was not as if prospective candidates held off in the expectation that Cadman would be easily reindorsed.

When Joe Hockey resigned from North Sydney after Malcolm Turnbull named him as ambassador to Washington in September 2015, there were only three candidates for preselection, and that in a seat where Hockey had enjoyed a majority of 16 per cent at the previous election. Six years before that, after Brendan Nelson retired from Bradfield, which for most of the previous 50 years had been the party's safest seat in New South Wales, the preselection for a replacement candidate drew 16 nominees, a number closer to those of earlier years.

In the months before the 2016 election, Philip Ruddock indicated that he would not seek to recontest his seat of Berowra at that election. Berowra boasted a Liberal majority of close to 20 per cent, one of the best on offer. Yet only three people sought Liberal endorsement, including Julian Leeser, the present MP. He was an excellent successor to Ruddock. Highly intelligent, he had been active in the party organisation in Berowra, constantly building its membership, conducting public forums on topical issues and generally reaching out to the community. He set an example that many would do well to follow.

Thirty years earlier there would have been many more than three candidates seeking the Liberal nod, but a Julian Leeser type would still have won, because he or she would have appealed to the electorate through a combination of high intelligence and energetic branch development. The difference would have been that back then the Liberal Party was seen as more open and genuinely competitive. A lot more people would have thought they had a chance.

The entrenchment of factions can lead to preselection challenges of a totemic kind that have no purpose other than to replace a parliamentarian of a particular stripe with someone of another. An attempt to do this occurred during the last 18 months of my prime ministership. Senator Marise Payne, the former Foreign Minister, was a prominent member of the small-l Liberal faction in New South Wales, and during 2006 a rival group in that state began organising a preselection challenge to her position. This rival group had a majority on the New South Wales Executive. I met their leaders, which included Senator Concetta Fierravanti-Wells, as well as State President Nick Campbell, who confirmed that a challenge to Payne was being contemplated. When I asked why they wanted to remove her, Fierravanti-Wells said that they 'wanted her replaced by a more conservative person'. When pressed, they volunteered the names of some long-standing party people who had given a lot to our cause. I knew they would not make any greater mark in the Senate than Marise Payne, and thus justify the upheaval involved in throwing out a serving senator. Her replacement would be seen for what it was: the product of ongoing factional warfare.

I told them that there was no benefit to the party in Payne's removal and that it would only intensify internal party friction in the lead-up to an election. Fortunately, common sense prevailed and the challenge to Payne was called off. But it had taken my personal involvement, and other arm-twisting and appeals to the greater good.

Some of the same factional issues attended the experience of Mike Baird, the former Premier of New South Wales. In 2005, before he entered state parliament, he expressed an interest in obtaining Liberal preselection for the state seat of Manly. I was PM at the time and was enthusiastic about Baird. He was a Manly local, and had enjoyed a very successful career at a young age in the financial community. In New South Wales the Liberals had languished in opposition for a decade. To me he was precisely the type of new candidate needed to increase the party's appeal in that state.

In conversation one day, I asked his father, Bruce, who still served in federal parliament as the MP for Cook, how his son's preselection pursuit was faring. Bruce said that Mike was probably going to abandon it, because 'the right who control the numbers in that area want someone else'. That someone else was well known as part of the more conservative section of the party. He was not of the same calibre as Baird. But Manly was 'theirs'. I thought this was appalling. As Manly was within the federal electorate of Warringah, held by Tony Abbott, then Health Minister, I urged him to use his influence on the relevant branches in Manly to swing behind Baird. Apparently, they did, as Baird stayed in the contest, took out the preselection and went on to become Premier.

It is denying reality for any member of the Liberal Party in New South Wales to pretend that factions have not crowded out more broadly based decision-making in relation to party affairs. Factions not only adopt positions on potential parliamentary candidates, but will also caucus on administrative issues, including the choice of senior staff.

Some draw satisfaction from the fact that such developments mirror what has occurred perennially within the ALP. In doing so they seem to completely ignore the fact that our opponents believe that the rights and interests of the individual should always be subjugated to those of the collective. As I argue in 'The Broad Church', *we* are meant to be different.

The saga of Kristina Keneally's preferment in 2022 as the ALP candidate for the previously ultra-safe Labor seat of Fowler is a case study of how factionalism works to the detriment of any semblance of a democratic process. To start with, under Labor protocols, the party leadership can suspend a local vote for any seat it chooses. Secondly, a factional understanding gives the top slot on the ALP Senate ticket for New South Wales to someone from one faction and the second to someone from another faction, and the third reverts to someone else from the first faction. Keneally was imposed on the Fowler electorate because she was likely to lose to another member of her faction in a ballot for the top Senate slot and was told she would have to 'accept' the third slot on the ALP ticket, which electoral history suggested the ALP (and thus Keneally) would probably not win.

This all happened because Keneally's faction was dominant in the New South Wales ALP. The views of the local ALP members in Fowler were contemptuously ignored. The brutal cynicism of the whole exercise was an affront to democracy.

In probably the most spectacular outcome in an individual seat on 21 May, Keneally was defeated in Fowler by a local resident of Vietnamese descent who ran as an independent. The Labor Party paid the ultimate price for arrogantly taking for granted the Fowler locals.

The methods used for selecting candidates in the Liberal Party vary somewhat between divisions. In 2018 the New South Wales Division decided to move to a plebiscite system involving all branch members. Most other divisions have a like approach. I strongly supported the change in New South Wales, which was hard fought, as some of the self-appointed factional chieftains feared they would lose influence under the system finally adopted.

The strength of the new system is that every single party member (after a qualifying period for a new member) has a vote in choosing the party's candidate in the electorate in which the member is involved. I can think of no greater direct incentive for a person to become involved in the Liberal Party than to be able to have a direct and equal say in choosing the party's candidates. This is particularly relevant in those electorates which have been regarded over the years as safe for the Liberal Party.

It is instructive that in the lead-up to the last federal election there was considerable resentment that the full plebiscite preselection system was in several cases put to one side. The party membership liked the inherently democratic nature of the recently implemented preselection system. They were angry that special privileges were extended to sitting MPs.

It is almost 49 years since I was chosen as the Liberal candidate for Bennelong by a panel with a maximum of 50 participants. The party then had a larger membership, had greater diversity of opinion and was infinitely less factionalised than it is now. Such a small selection panel would no longer be appropriate for today's Liberal Party. I faced 24 other aspirants for that seat. Today the number of aspirants for a safe Liberal electorate would be far fewer.

A party that claims to believe in market forces must accept that this means talented men and women will be discouraged from nominating themselves in the belief that a tightly held factional system gives them little chance of winning.

Over time the plebiscite system should change those perceptions.

Putnam's analysis in *Bowling Alone* was broadly accurate. In Australia, the baby boomer generation and the one before it, of which I am a member, were the last 'joiner' generations. The consequences for political parties are inescapable. Less diverse party membership means that there is less natural resistance to zealous activists' intent to bring about group dominance or factional control.

CHOOSING THE LEADER

Reflections on balancing polls and
policy in party leadership change

When Scott Morrison was sworn in as Australia's PM in September 2018, he was the fifth person to occupy that position since my defeat by Kevin Rudd in November 2007. He lost the election in May 2022 to Anthony Albanese, who will need to win again – likely in an election in 2025 – to be the first incumbent prime minister to win re-election after serving a full term as prime minister since my victory in 2004, some 20 years earlier.

By any measure there has been a remarkable turnover in the leadership of our Federal Government in the past 11 years. There were six PMs between the retirement of Robert Menzies in 1966 and Fraser's election nine years later, but two resulted from the death by drowning of Harold Holt; his immediate successor, John McEwen, was only a caretaker while the Liberal Party chose John Gorton, who became the next PM.

Changes in opposition leadership are expected, and to an extent seen as commonplace. What has made the past 11 years so remarkable is that four of the changes involved the removal of a serving PM by his or her party. Labor PM Kevin Rudd was replaced by Julia Gillard, who in turn was replaced by a returning Rudd. Liberal PM Tony Abbott was replaced by Malcolm Turnbull, who was later replaced by Scott Morrison.

The contrast with the previous generation is stark. The ALP was in power for 13 years: under Bob Hawke for seven and a half years and then Paul Keating for a little over four. In the end, their leadership struggle had been fierce, but conventional; the younger long-serving Treasurer and deputy wanted his turn, and the older hugely successful leader was running out of puff. It was a stable period of government. Many regard it as probably the most successful Labor government in our history. Whitlam commanded greater affection among the Labor faithful, but Hawke delivered more votes.

After the ALP's heavy defeat in 1996, the Howard Government was in power for almost 12 years. There were no leadership challenges and, in the only case since federation, the same three people occupied the three most significant positions for the duration of the government: me as PM, Peter Costello as Treasurer and Alexander Downer as Foreign Minister. Reinforcing that was the solidity of the Coalition, due in no small measure to the skill and loyalty of three successive National leaders, Tim Fischer, John Anderson and Mark Vaile.

That aggregate period of 25 years saw a lot of economic reform, with plenty of bipartisanship, but only from the Coalition. Labor, in opposition after 1996, never returned the compliment, an issue I take up in 'Bipartisanship: A One-way Street'. Although the political contest continued unabated, Australia enjoyed 25 years of political stability.

Until Tony Abbott was toppled, the only previous occasion on which the Liberals had removed an incumbent PM was when, in 1971, Bill McMahon replaced John Gorton. It was anything but an emphatic change of captain: the vote of confidence in Gorton was a deadlock and Gorton delivered a casting vote against himself. Yet it had a considerable history.

When Gorton became PM after the death of Harold Holt, he inherited a substantial majority. He lost a swag of seats at the next election in 1969 but survived a leadership challenge from McMahon and National Development Minister David Fairbairn. The outcome of the 1970 half-Senate election was dismal. Gorton was regularly at war with the long-serving Liberal premiers of the two largest states, New South Wales and Victoria.

Increasingly present amid the growing dissatisfaction with Gorton was the belief that he was a centralist and had little patience with the federalist philosophy dear to many Liberals. Those Liberals regarded the division of power within a federation as a core belief. To them he had ridden roughshod over something that was part of the essence of what the party stood for. John Gorton was a passionate Australian nationalist and, although some of the criticism directed against him was justified, he frequently and rightly saw insistence on the rights of the states as hindering the achievement of desirable national goals. Not unnaturally, as a prime minister myself, I largely thought in terms of national goals and aspirations.

Going back a few years earlier, John McEwen's refusal to serve under Bill McMahon if he became Liberal leader, after Harold Holt's death in 1967, will long be remembered as the most dramatic ever use of power to influence a leadership contest within the Liberal Party, albeit by the leader of the Country (now National) Party.

Despite the emphasis regularly placed on the personal difficulties between Bill McMahon and his ministerial colleagues, McEwen's veto on McMahon was fundamentally about policy. John McEwen was a protectionist, McMahon more instinctively a free trader. They often clashed over Tariff Board decisions. They squared off over the level of the exchange rate when it was fixed by the government and not the market. The Country Party icon was widely admired in Coalition circles, partly because of the vision he had shown in achieving the commerce agreement with Japan in 1957. He was seen as a powerful advocate for Australian interests abroad.

McMahon was deeply distrusted by his colleagues. Yet this unpopularity tended to mask the depth of the policy differences between him and McEwen. In essence, they disagreed about the level of government involvement in the running of the economy. As discussed in 'Bipartisanship: A One-way Street', that issue would lie at the heart of the economic debate for decades to follow, not only in Australia but around the world: barely a trivial matter. Their poor personal relations intensified their policy differences, and vice versa.

If the two momentous leadership stand-offs involving first Bill McMahon and then John Gorton involved fundamental policy matters, as I have stated, no such policy considerations governed the replacement of Rudd by Gillard, Gillard by Rudd, Abbott by Turnbull or Turnbull by Morrison.

Nothing resembling the issues behind John Gorton's removal was present in September 2015 when the party pulled down Tony Abbott. Less than two years previously, Abbott had led the Coalition to a convincing victory, securing a majority of 30 seats in the House of Representatives.

At the 2010 election, Abbott had gone within an ace of toppling a first-term government. Yet all that was now cast aside because Abbott was behind in the polls.

Famously, Malcolm Turnbull cited the Coalition deficit in 30 preceding Newspolls as a major reason why Abbott should be removed. At no point, though, was a coherent policy case advanced as to why Abbott should be deposed. It was not as if MPs were outraged by Abbott's repudiation of a fundamental tenet of Liberal philosophy. Many Liberals who later disdained Turnbull would point to Turnbull's loss of even more than 30 Newspolls as a reason why *he* should go.

Significantly, two of the issues on which Abbott and Turnbull most strongly disagreed, namely same-sex marriage and the monarchy, were free vote areas for the Liberals. Abbott and Turnbull had different views on climate change, and Turnbull's stance on that issue had been instrumental in his removal as opposition leader in 2009. Yet in 2015, Abbott's climate change beliefs were not nominated by Turnbull as a major reason why Abbott should go. The principal indictment Turnbull presented was Abbott's supposed inability to argue economic issues effectively. It is probable that most Liberals did not share Malcolm Turnbull's opinions on climate change when they installed him as PM.

I thought in 2010, and still do, that Labor made a huge blunder in replacing Rudd with Gillard. Again, although there were plenty of stories to the effect that he had poor working relations with his colleagues, I was not conscious that Rudd had been removed because of a major policy disagreement. That was not asserted at the time. The best explanation that the freshly installed Julia Gillard could offer was that 'a good government was losing its way'.[1]

The removal of two PMs who had led their parties back into government before either had completed a full term bespoke immaturity and an incapacity to treat politics seriously. Polls are often bad for incumbent governments. I can testify to that. Even on that score, the Newspoll just before Rudd's removal was 52–48 Labor's way!

These recent leadership changes have been driven more by personality trivia and factionalism, and that, as argued in the previous two essays, the character of parliamentary parties within our political system has undergone basic change during the 40-year period that separates these events from those involving McMahon and Gorton.

The high turnover of PMs during the past 11 years has prompted plenty of introspection and debate about the way parliamentary leaders are chosen. The ALP, at the instance of Kevin Rudd when he returned to the prime ministership in 2013, embraced a hybrid system involving the general party membership as well as the parliamentary members and senators. Under the new system equal weighting is given to the separate votes of the entire party membership and the parliamentary party. In 2013 Bill Shorten defeated Anthony Albanese in the contest for the party leadership because his victory among the parliamentary membership was greater than Albanese's victory among the rank and file.

The Liberal Party, wisely in my view, has not included the general membership in leadership ballots. The only change that has been made was in December 2018, when the parliamentary party resolved that in future a Liberal PM could not be removed from the party leadership during the entirety of his or her immediate term. The one exception would be a no-confidence motion carried against an incumbent by a two-thirds majority: an extremely unlikely scenario. If that proviso had been in place in 2013 Tony Abbott would likely not have been removed, nor would Malcolm Turnbull have fallen in 2018. If it had applied in 1971, John Gorton would probably have remained PM.

I strongly oppose any change to party voting rules that would dilute the total control MPs have over the election of their leaders. In a Westminster system, the most important relationship a leader has is with the people he or she immediately leads: the senators and MPs who comprise the parliamentary party. It is important for the leader to have good relations with his or her party organisation, and be fully involved in its many activities, but the daily contact is with his or her parliamentary colleagues. Nothing comparable exists even in the relationship between the parliamentary leader and the Federal President of the Liberal Party.

The relationship the leader shares with his or her parliamentary colleagues is quite an intimate one. The effectiveness of this relationship will determine whether the person in charge stands or falls. MPs daily observe how the leader responds to constant pressure. When parliament sits the interaction is regular and often very intense, and it occurs in the context of the daily political contest with the other side of politics. The remarkably close nature of the relationship means that character can be clearly observed.

When I led the Liberal Party, in both government and opposition, I received immeasurable support from the party organisation, and most particularly the four successive federal directors with whom I worked, Tony Eggleton, Andrew Robb, Lynton Crosby and Brian Loughnane. To all of them I owe a great debt. But their assistance and advice were always predicated on the settled understanding between the organisation and the parliamentary party: what I describe in the next chapter as an 'implied covenant'. A federal director would from time to time convey the wider party's views, sometimes angry and restless, about a particular policy or political failure within the parliamentary party, but never in a way that challenged the understanding between the parliamentarians and the lay party members.

The only occasion I can recall on which there was an open breach of this long-standing agreement in relation to the leadership was on the eve of the ballot between John Hewson and Alexander Downer in 1994, when the Federal President, Tony Staley, publicly called on the parliamentarians to vote Hewson out. It was an isolated personal intervention and did not suggest a broad shift by the party organisation towards overt intervention in choosing the party leader.

As stated, the nature of a parliamentary system is that members of the parliamentary party are uniquely placed to observe, assess and judge their colleagues, because they have in common the distinction of having been chosen through a democratic process to sit in parliament and make laws that affect all citizens. They have a special privilege, and that privilege should not be shared with other citizens who have not been chosen through the same process. Once a political party allows anyone other than duly elected MPs to become part of the process of selecting a party leader, it does in some way corrupt the democratic process.

The power the party membership has is the decisive one of choosing who their candidates will be. If they do not like the performance of any of their candidates who have won election to parliament, they can take away their party endorsements, but they should never usurp the role those candidates have been elected to discharge.

The foregoing, however valid, is theoretical. To strike a more political note, it is worth casting more widely to the experience of the British Conservative Party. There are significant differences, but links between the Liberals and their British centre-right counterparts have always been close, thus rendering comparisons useful.

Edward 'Ted' Heath, who became British PM in 1970, was the first democratically elected leader of the Conservative Party. Prior to that, the leader emerged from a process that owed a lot to reverence for the opinions of party elders and men in grey or indeed other-coloured suits. Sometimes the process produced real surprises, such as the emergence of Alec Douglas-Home to replace Harold Macmillan as PM in 1963. The grandees did not want senior party figures Rab Butler and Iain Macleod, so they chose a Scottish peer, who had to find a seat in the Commons.

Partly as a result, the party resolved to have a proper ballot after Home resigned following the loss to Labour under Harold Wilson in 1964. Heath won that ballot, which was confined to MPs. After Heath lost two elections to Wilson in 1974, he was challenged by Margaret Thatcher, who knocked him out of the contest on the first ballot. She won on the next ballot. At that time the wider party membership was probably more sympathetic to Heath. They were not necessarily anti-Thatcher, but there was a natural loyalty to an incumbent leader who had been PM. They had been through battles together. They felt comfortable with Heath. By contrast, the MPs had seen both close at hand. They admired Thatcher's pugnacious spirit and debating skills. To them she was the future, and they backed her.

The relevance of this is that after Tony Blair had won the 1997 election for Labour, William Hague, the Conservatives' new leader, sponsored a revised system to choose the Conservative Party leader thereafter. Under the new system, the parliamentary party would winnow the choice down to two, and then ask the entire party membership to make the final decision. It was this process that led David Cameron to become Conservative leader and Boris Johnson to become Conservative leader and PM. If that two-stage system had been in operation in 1975, Margaret Thatcher might have had a much tougher fight to defeat Heath. Many in the general party membership would have backed Heath, out of loyalty to an incumbent, ahead of the person who went on to become such a remarkable and hugely successful PM.

When, incredibly enough, the British Labour Party chose Jeremy Corbyn as its leader, the overwhelming consensus was that he would be trounced at any election. He was a bitter socialist throw-back to the class-driven politics of an earlier era, completely repudiating the approach of Tony Blair, who had delivered the Labour Party a decade of government. He became leader, unexpectedly, after a rule change sponsored by the previous leader, Ed Miliband. This change allowed any self-declared supporter of the party on payment of five pounds to vote in the leadership ballot, and helped Corbyn win comfortably.

Shamefully, Corbyn had at best allowed the evil of anti-Semitism to spread in his party. A clumsy campaign by Theresa May in 2017 gave Corbyn a brief commutation, but in 2019 he was roundly defeated by Boris Johnson. Yet for several years he was the alternative PM of Great Britain.

A footnote to this narrative is to recall the circumstances in which Britain's greatest ever PM, Winston Churchill, became the King's first minister. He emerged from the massive uncertainty following the heavy defection of Conservative MPs in a crucial House of Commons vote at a critical time in May 1940. Confidence in Neville Chamberlain as PM had evaporated. Many Conservatives were against Churchill; they probably preferred Lord Halifax, the pro-appeasement Foreign Secretary. There had even been some moves in Churchill's constituency to remove his party's endorsement of him. Labour and the Liberals tended to favour Churchill over other Tory alternatives. The King was believed to favour Halifax, who in the end was reluctant to serve. From all this, the final advice to the monarch was to send for Churchill and ask him to form a government. This advice, which was to prove so wise, came out of the mystical process, incapable of proper definition, that would continue to surround the way in which the Conservative establishment chose political leaders up until Ted Heath's election. The final irony was that after Churchill became PM, Chamberlain remained leader of the Conservative Party until his death some months later, when Churchill took on that role. These were exceptional circumstances that yielded a remarkable leader. Appropriately enough, they do not fit any neat formula.

During my almost 12 years as PM, I was not involved in any leadership ballots. There were none, either for the leadership or the deputy leadership; this reflected the great stability of that period.

It had been very different in opposition. There had been plenty then.

I have often reflected that the first time I became Liberal leader was by accident, and it was ended by an ambush. As case studies in how to handle leadership change, both were instructive in how *not* to do it.

In September 1985, most of my parliamentary colleagues did not want to remove Andrew Peacock as leader of the party. He had outperformed most expectations at the December 1984 election, winning seats from Bob Hawke and besting him in the leaders' debate. Equally, a majority did not agree with him that someone else should replace me as deputy leader. Largely because of my five years as Treasurer, I spoke with far greater authority on economic issues than anyone else in the Coalition.

Because Andrew had pressed for me to step down as deputy, he felt he had to resign when the party voted to *keep* me as deputy. It was an unsatisfactory situation, to say the least. The result was an outcome that settled nothing. I remained, for less than an hour, as deputy. Then I was elected leader to fill a vacancy that the party had not wanted.

The aftermath of this unexpected change in 1985 was lingering bitterness and deep division. Those close to Andrew resented my becoming leader and argued that it was all my fault for not having accepted his authority. Those close to *me* claimed that it had all happened because Andrew had made an unreasonable demand of me. There was merit on both sides, but what could not be disputed was that the party suffered as a result.

Those within the Liberal Party who argued for *my* removal in May 1989 took advantage of the adverse opinion polls in their private canvassing of undecided senators and MPs. Because it was an ambush, their campaign was conducted in great secrecy. The suddenness of the coup was a surprise to me and to many of my parliamentary colleagues. Some of the post-coup boasting by the plotters angered ordinary party members.

Democracy only works if everyone accepts the result, even if the minority had wished it to be otherwise. Only in a technical sense did everyone accept the result of 5 September 1985 that delivered me the leadership of the Liberal Party. In an emotional sense they did not, for the simple reason that it was not a majority decision, but an accidental result. If there had been a ballot for the leadership between Peacock and me that day, he would have won it.

Leadership contests can be bitterly fought and only narrowly concluded, but nonetheless accepted. The contest between Hawke and Keating in December 1991 was one such. It was the culmination of an intense struggle, resulting in the pulling down of the ALP's most successful leader ever. Yet it was conclusive, confirmed by Hawke's decision to leave parliament shortly afterwards. There was to be no return bout.

When one of the participants in a leadership contest draws stumps and departs, or his or her time has clearly come and gone, there is a mood of finality that is important for longer-term stability. On the other hand, if the defeated contestant stays in the ring and is seen as a continuing rival, particularly when the party is obviously divided on policy issues and the two recent antagonists represent the different viewpoints, then a sense of unfinished leadership business remains.

After I became leader in 1985, Andrew Peacock continued in parliament, and there was a strong and quite natural sense that he could well return to the leadership. Even more did Kevin Rudd remain as a potential rival to Julia Gillard. The pressure this placed on her after the 2010 election was massive, and she finally succumbed. The rivalry between Tony Abbott and Malcolm Turnbull never really ended until they had both, in turn, been removed from the prime ministership by their own party.

When it became known that I had played some role in persuading Turnbull to stay in parliament in 2009 after Abbott had taken the leadership from him, I was criticised by those close to Abbott. They had dearly hoped that Turnbull would leave the reservation entirely, for the simple reason that he was seen as a continuing threat to Abbott. After all, Abbott's victory by just one vote had been utterly unexpected. The consensus opinion had been that Joe Hockey would replace Turnbull, but Hockey blew it through his extraordinary proposal to allow Liberal MPs a conscience vote on whether to support Rudd's emissions trading scheme. It was a core economic issue and the Coalition had to settle on a clear policy and unite behind it.

Although Turnbull's first instinct was to quit politics, he had every reason to stay around. Given the subsequent electoral history of Wentworth, which is now held by Allegra Spender, who took the seat from David Sharma at the 2022 May election, it should be noted that the Liberal Party organisation did not want Turnbull to leave parliament as they feared the seat would go to an independent in a by-election. The tension between him and Abbott never really abated; the mistrust was too deeply entrenched. Finally, in a ballot conducted on 14 September 2015, Turnbull defeated Abbott for the leadership.

The 2016 election saw Turnbull go within an ace of losing by forfeiting 14 seats of the handsome majority Abbott had won three years earlier. The next day I spent an hour on the phone with the narrowly re-elected PM. Among other things, I tried to persuade him to make Tony Abbott Defence Minister. He refused on the ground that he couldn't trust him. Such a move would not have quenched Abbott's desire to return to the Lodge, but it would have given the country an energetic and articulate Defence Minister, with a deep commitment to our defence personnel. It would also have kept Abbott within the tent. Instead, he remained a restless, discontented soul on the backbench, a constant irritant to Turnbull.

There are cases when a leadership change is validated by an impressive election victory, and the continued presence in parliament of the former leader presents no threat. The two prominent examples in my time in parliament were Malcolm Fraser's defeat of Billy Snedden in March 1975, and Bill Hayden's replacement by Bob Hawke early in 1983.

So accepting was Snedden of Fraser's electoral win with a record majority in December 1975 that he opted to run for the speakership, which he easily secured and retained for the duration of the Fraser Government. After Hawke won government in March 1983 Snedden joined the mass parliamentary exit of his generation of Coalition colleagues.

Bob Hawke's big win entrenched his position as Labor leader. Hayden was well treated by his Labor colleagues, who had clinically cut him down despite all the work he had done to restore the ALP's reputation after much of the chaos of the Whitlam years. I liked Bill Hayden, and it was impossible not to feel sorry for him when he was replaced by Hawke. We can never know whether Hayden, like the drover's dog he invoked, would have beaten Fraser in 1983. What we do know is that Hawke's elevation to the leadership sealed the fate of the Coalition.

Hawke successively made Hayden Minister for Foreign Affairs, then Governor-General. Prime ministers have the capacity to appoint people to a variety of positions. No such options are available to opposition leaders.

THE BROAD CHURCH

Reflections on the balance of political traditions
within the Liberal Party of Australia

Before I became PM, and during my time in the Lodge, I regularly argued that the Liberal Party of Australia, unlike many other centre-right parties around the world, was the custodian of two traditions within the Australian polity. They were the classical liberal tradition and the conservative tradition. I described the Liberal Party as a broad church.

That expression was originally used to depict the breadth of doctrinal and liturgical opinion and practice within the Anglican Church, from its 'high' or Anglo-Catholic stream to its 'low' or evangelical iteration. In using the expression, I was not identifying the party in any way with the Church and its beliefs, but rather observing echoes between the breadth of conviction within the Anglican Church and that within the political party I had joined in 1957.

In the 65 years I have been a member of the Liberal Party, I have carefully followed the interplay of ideology and policy within it. I have observed the influence of both conservative and liberal philosophies, and witnessed attempts by some to characterise the party as either wholly one or the other. I have rejected these attempts, believing that our party is a genuine composite of both conservatism and liberalism, and is more effective politically when identified as such.

In this chapter I reflect on this idea by reference to the party's experience in both government and opposition.

Political descriptions or labels promote endless debate and often much confusion. Certain words carry different meanings in different countries. The most obvious example is the word 'liberal' itself. In a political context, its meaning in the US is virtually the opposite of that in Australia.

For want of a better description, a liberal in the US is someone to the left of centre, who typically believes in more rather than less government involvement in the affairs of people and in the operation of the economy. The Democratic Party is the natural home of most American liberals. By contrast, those who oppose too much government, have far stronger free-market inclinations and identify more openly with business would see themselves as being on the centre-right of politics, and would normally call themselves 'conservatives'. Their natural home would customarily be the Republican Party.

In recent decades, as debates on social issues have intensified, most American liberals have more strongly supported such things as the relaxation of abortion laws and the legalisation of same-sex marriage. It is probable that the bulk of conservatives have been less enthusiastic about such changes.

These are broad generalisations. There are numerous exceptions to the rule, but not so many as to render the generalisations inaccurate.

It is important to appreciate the differences in American society that have shaped its politics. The government plays a lesser support role in America than is the case in Australia, and even less so than in Europe. Many activities that are assumed as responsibilities by the state in Australia are carried by private interests in the US. I was surprised to learn some years ago that Central Park in New York is operated and maintained by a private trust. Physical mail deliveries are government-owned and –operated but, before they were superseded, telegraphic services were private. The same can be said of rail services. There have never been major debates about privatisation in the US, for the simple reason that there are fewer government-owned assets available to sell off.

The US fought a terrible civil war that claimed more lives than the nation has lost in total in all the military conflicts in which it has subsequently been involved. This bloody conflict directly involved the rights of the states. It has left a permanent mistrust of government in many parts of the country. This is an ever-present sentiment in most American political debate. Australians may sneer at their politicians from time to time, but there is never the level of visceral hostility to the state here that is so often encountered in the US. This is not to be confused with the hand-on-heart patriotism of most Americans, which expresses a love of country, as distinct from a love of the instruments of state.

The southern states of the United States became a bastion of the Democratic Party after the Civil War, because Abraham Lincoln, a Republican, had led the victorious Union in the North. This would change dramatically in the 1960s, when Lyndon Johnson, a Democrat, drove civil rights reforms through Congress. The South opposed both the pace and much of the substance of these long-needed reforms. Since then, the Republicans have usually bested the Democrats in much of the old southern Confederacy.

When we use the word 'liberal' in Australia, we not only think of the party that bears that name, but also of the classical liberal tradition that originated in Britain and is identified with people such as John Stuart Mill. It places great emphasis on the individual and his or her liberties. Liberalism has always championed freedom of speech, worship and association. To classical liberals, the collective will never smother the individual. It is a tradition that has opposed distinctions based on class; it has sought to judge people according to their contribution to society, and to see them promoted according to merit. It strongly supports free enterprise.

For well over 100 years, the major political contest in Britain was between the Liberal Party (once known as the Whigs) and the Conservative Party (still often called the Tories). Over time the Liberal Party was effectively squeezed between the rise of the British Labour Party, which attracted massive working-class and trade union support, and the Conservatives.

The British Labour Party has contained many who are classical liberals. I regarded Tony Blair as one. He was not a product of his party's trade union roots and was a world away from Labour politicians such as post-World War II Welsh firebrand Aneurin Bevan, Health Minister in the Attlee Government, or even Harold Wilson, Prime Minister in the 1960s and 1970s.

What this brief analysis tells us is that although political parties all have distinctive features, they cannot be neatly grouped according to specific ideological beliefs, with lines of demarcation that are never blurred. They are all creatures of history, often shaped by momentous debates on major issues or shifted by great national upheavals.

All political parties are in some way coalitions. This is even more so in societies such as Australia's, in which divisions along class lines are less evident. The large size of the Australian middle class, principally the product of our relative income equality, has meant that political allegiances often straddle the classes, such that those classes might continue to exist. In the 1950s it was broadly accurate to say that the great bulk of the working class voted for the ALP, with the rest divided, although with a tilt towards the Liberals. One caveat was that many Catholics who by no means remained working class continued to support the Labor Party, seemingly out of tribal habit. This would change dramatically in the 1960s, after Menzies championed state aid for independent schools, which (as explained in the Introduction) was of particular benefit to Catholic schools. This accelerated probably the greatest demographic shift in Australian politics of the post-World War II era. The Liberal Party that I joined in the late 1950s was overwhelmingly Protestant. When I lost office in 2007, precisely half of the outgoing cabinet identified as Catholics.

Attempts to clearly define the Liberal Party as being predominantly a conservative one, or a classically liberal one, are destined to fail because neither fits the facts. As I said, it is in so many ways a broad church. My long experience in the party has taught me that its unity, and ultimately its effectiveness, depend upon accommodating both strains of opinion within its broad philosophical base.

Certainly, the attitudes of Robert Menzies, our party's

founder, reveal a mixture of conservative and classical liberal views on a wide range of subjects.

In recent years, it has been a constant refrain of some small-l Liberals that theirs is the true Menzies tradition. They have emphasised the fact that Menzies chose the name 'Liberal' when he formed the party in 1944, and have drawn on our founder's explanation that 'We took the name "Liberal" because we were determined to be a progressive party, willing to make experiments, in no sense reactionary but believing in the individual, his rights, and his enterprise, and rejecting the socialist panacea.'

In invoking the name of Menzies in this way, they have attributed to him attitudes not supported by many historical facts. Menzies and all of those who have followed him as leaders have held fast *classical* liberalism as their broad philosophical base. They have valued the individual ahead of the collective, and they have embraced free enterprise and supported freedom of speech, worship and association.

Menzies governed in very different times, and in many specific ways he was both an economic and a social conservative. He was a staunch supporter of the monarchy and showed no inclination to alter the social order. On the specifics of economic policy, he can fairly be described as a conservative. As I argue in the next chapter, he subscribed to the Keynesian consensus, reinforcing the policies that had been so successful in the past.

The same could be said of his approach to foreign policy. The cornerstone of his attitude was our alliances with the United States and Britain, and he strongly supported his government's crucial 1957 trade agreement with Japan, little more than a decade after the hostilities of World War II. He was careful about major changes in immigration policy, and it took Harold Holt to finally dismantle the White Australia policy. Menzies's 1963 initiative on state aid for independent and Catholic schools was radical at the time, but utterly consistent with his liberal principles.

As PM, some of the strongest criticism I received within the Liberal Party over asylum seekers and border protection came from MPs and others who identified as small-l Liberals. From time to time a few of their number would mutter something to the effect of 'Menzies would not have endorsed that approach'.

It was, of course, impossible to know. Nonetheless, it *was* possible to know what Menzies did in circumstances of his time that pitted the rights of certain individuals against what was then judged to be the national interest.

The prime example was his vigorous attempts to ban the Communist Party of Australia, ultimately through the referendum of September 1951. It was called because legislation passed the previous year outlawing the Communist Party had been declared by the High Court to be beyond parliament's constitutional power.

That referendum split the nation. My father voted Yes, but my mother voted No. It was the only occasion I am aware of when they voted differently. Ultimately the referendum failed, in part at least on civil liberties grounds. Menzies's proposal was draconian, yet it occurred at a time of global concern about the threat of Soviet-led communism, and less than two years after the Communist takeover in China. Australian troops were fighting alongside their American, British and South Korean allies against the invading North Koreans, allied with the Chinese. Communist union officials also held disproportionate influence in key Australian industries.

In the long run, the issue caused more harm to Labor than the Liberal Party (as touched on in 'Bowling Alone'). Yet some Liberals broke ranks to oppose Menzies, accusing him of trampling on free speech. One of those was the late Alan Missen, then a leading Victorian Young Liberal, later a senator from that state. A principled man, Missen was always firmly identified with the small-l Liberal disposition of the party.

When Menzies founded the Liberal Party of Australia, his aims were quite different from those that the small-l Liberals have attributed to him. The party was formed against the backdrop of disarray within anti-Labor ranks. The 1943 election had been a humiliation for the disintegrating United Australia Party, the main standard-bearer for conservatives at that time, led by the ageing and irascible Billy Hughes, political hero of World War I but now well past his time. Menzies's greatest gift to the Liberal cause was the genius he displayed in forming a new party from disparate anti-Labor groups, but based on the central role of the individual, and a resolute commitment to free enterprise. By 1944, through powerful advocacy and force of personality and intellect, he had gathered the shattered forces and put together the Liberal Party.

In 1947, as opposition leader, he grabbed hold of Labor Prime Minister Ben Chifley's disastrous and blatantly socialistic policy of nationalising the private trading banks. In doing so, he consolidated his hold on the still-infant Liberal Party. It would become the most successful party in Australia's history.

Many things about this new party were different from its predecessors. For one thing, there was what the late John Carrick, one of the greatest servants the party has ever had, called an 'implied covenant'. This meant that the parliamentary party was supreme in matters of policy, and the organisation had its own entirely separate responsibilities. Each would zealously guard its turf.

In marking out the freedom of the parliamentary party from any semblance of outside control, Menzies showed his consummate political wisdom. Not only was the implied covenant right in principle, but it also worked greatly to the Liberal Party's political advantage.

By contrast, the domination of Labor MPs by the party organisation and the trade union movement would become a defining issue in the 1960s. In probably the most iconic domestic political photograph of that decade, Labor parliamentary leader Arthur Calwell and his deputy Gough Whitlam were pictured in 1963 outside the Kingston Hotel in Canberra, speaking to a senior official of their party. This official was describing what was happening at no less than a special meeting of the National Executive of the ALP. That meeting would determine the party's policy towards the communications centre at North West Cape in Western Australia, a vital link in the defensive network of the United States. Australia's involvement was an important earnest of our close anti-communist alliance with the Americans.

The 36 members of the National Executive of the ALP could dictate policy on any issue. Incredibly, Calwell and Whitlam were not members of the executive, so they could not attend the meeting. The symbolism of a picture that captured them waiting under a Canberra lamppost to be told what their policy would be by unelected party officials was devastating. Bob Menzies could hardly believe his luck. That photograph and what it represented haunted the ALP for years, with the Liberal PM and his colleagues constantly taunting their opponents with references to the '36 faceless men'.

Historically, the ALP has always demanded greater adherence to the collective decisions of the party. A culture in which loyalty to the group decision is more important than individual conscience is barely surprising in a party spawned by the trade union movement.

Discipline in the Labor Party has always been tighter, expulsion a constant threat for those who did not comply. To be a Labor 'rat' was the most odious of epithets. Those who earned that title – most notoriously of all, Billy Hughes, PM from 1915 to 1923, first as leader of the Labor Party, then of the National Party – were never forgiven. In Hughes's case, the issue that separated him from the party he had embraced for decades was hardly trivial. It was whether, at a desperate time for the Allies in 1917, the nation should introduce military conscription. As recently as 1995, Graeme Campbell, the Labor MP for Kalgoorlie, was effectively pushed out of the parliamentary party because he would not support aspects of Labor policy on native title. He resigned rather than be expelled, then won the seat as an independent at the 1996 election.

When Menzies formed the Liberal Party in 1944 he went to great lengths to insulate it from any form of external control, and internally, to mandate the freedom of MPs on policy issues. There were several organisational principles he embraced to protect it against maladies that had beset its anti-Labor predecessor, the United Australia Party.

For instance, fundraising was to be done by the organisation and kept out of the control of the MPs. Care was to be taken that industry groups did not control large donations. The support of individual companies would always be welcome, indeed solicited, but clusters of donors who might see themselves as exerting special influence on a particular issue were to be avoided.

There was to be a strong federal organisation, ensuring that a national perspective remained paramount. Finally, and most importantly, the quid pro quo for the policy freedom of the parliamentary party was that the party organisation would select party candidates. As the years passed that preserve was jealously guarded. In recent years, as argued in 'Bowling Alone', many party members have pushed the envelope on this. But Menzies always treated the organisation respectfully, as I did.

When Menzies was riding high in 1956, having won four elections in a row, the deputy Liberal leader, Eric Harrison, decided to retire. This necessitated a by-election in Harrison's seat of Wentworth. The party chose Leslie Bury as its candidate, Menzies making no secret of the fact that he wanted him.

Even though the full preselection protocols had been observed, there was a lot of local resentment towards Bury. He had served as a senior Treasury economist, and as Australia's representative on the International Monetary Fund and World Bank. Those appointments only go to top notches. Yet he was an outsider who, so the complaint ran, had been imposed on the local party by Menzies. The uproar in the electorate was such that three people ran as independent liberals, and Bury was forced to preferences, finally winning by 51.6 per cent to 48.4 per cent on a two-party-preferred basis. The grass roots had made their views known. Not even at the height of the 'Ming dynasty' could they be ignored. In those years, members of the Liberal Party could run against endorsed Liberal candidates without automatically imperilling their membership. In the 1960s this was tightened, so that automatic expulsion was visited upon those who stood or campaigned against endorsed Liberal candidates.

As opposition leader, I personally experienced the sensitivity of the party organisation to any perceived intervention by me in a preselection. In 1989, David Kemp, later a senior minister in my government, mounted a challenge against Ian Macphee, who was the sitting member for Goldstein, then a safe Liberal seat in Melbourne.

Macphee was a small-l Liberal, and a strong opponent of my views on many things, including industrial relations. Although we had entered parliament together in 1974, and had been ministerial colleagues in the Fraser Government, our relationship in opposition had not been easy. I had dropped him from my shadow ministry in 1987 – somewhat unwisely, as I would later reflect.

There was huge interest in the Goldstein contest; Malcolm Fraser strongly backed Macphee, even though

Kemp had once worked for the former PM. The media also supported Macphee, and pressure mounted on me to 'do something' to save him.

I had not in any way encouraged Kemp to nominate himself. I knew that his challenge had unnerved my colleagues, but I respected the right of the party organisation to adjudicate on the matter. Even if it was yet another element of instability, unhelpful to me at the time, my instincts were to stay out of the contest.

Rather tepidly, I telephoned Sir John (Bill) Anderson, a former Victorian party president, to inquire about the stoush. Anderson lived in Goldstein and was influential among the Liberals who would decide Macphee's fate. He was quite open and direct, telling me that several local Liberals had encouraged Kemp to nominate himself. Emphatically observing the implied covenant, he told me I should stay out of the preselection and leave it to the locals. Kemp went on to defeat Macphee in the preselection. Several days later I was removed from the leadership of the Liberal Party.

That term as opposition leader had been a turbulent one for me. It had included the destructive 'Joh for PM' campaign, which fractured the federal coalition with the National Party, and provided a clear illustration of the workings of the implied covenant between the organisation and the parliamentary party. It also shed light on the potential consequences for the Liberal Party of any weakening of the broad-church approach.

Joh Bjelke-Petersen was a classic conservative populist who, nonetheless, attracted a lot of investment to Queensland and oversaw strong economic growth in that state. He was always willing to take on militant unionism. Having governed in coalition with the Liberal Party for many years, the Bjelke-Petersen Nationals won a majority in their own right in the Queensland elections of 1986. This victory led him and others to believe that Joh had nationwide vote-winning appeal. Thus, was born the notion that he could become prime minister.

Bjelke-Petersen and most of the Queensland Nationals trenchantly criticised the federal coalition between the Liberals and the Nationals. Their threats to remove party endorsement from their Canberra senators and MPs effectively forced the Nationals out of a coalition that had successfully endured since World War II. It was an existential threat to the non-Labor side of politics.

Many of the renegade Nationals from Queensland railed against those they described as 'trendy Liberals'. There was a determined attempt to paint the Liberal Party as being out of touch with mainstream conservative thought. This charge had no substance and, as leader of the Liberals, I declared that I was the most conservative leader the party had ever had. I used those words to emphasise the centrality of conservative thought to the Liberal Party and certainly not to exclude classical liberalism from the mainstream philosophy of the party at that time. After all, it was the conservative roots of the party that were under attack, not its classical liberal values.

This crisis should serve as a reminder to all who wish the Liberal and National Parties well of what happens, and what political peril can face the two parties, and particularly the Liberals, when there is open division between, for want of another description, conservatives and liberals.

Within the Liberal Party at the time there was a range of opinions about how the relationship with the National Party should be handled. At no stage, though, was there any questioning of the prerogative of the parliamentary party concerning policy and parliamentary tactics. There was a universal acceptance within the leadership of the two parliamentary parties that whether the federal coalition continued should ultimately be a matter for the senators and MPs to decide.

It was the rogue action of the Queensland National Party organisation in threatening to withdraw endorsements from their Queensland senators and MPs that finally brought the coalition to an end and effectively delivered the 1987 election to Bob Hawke. Immediately after that election, because of the way the Queensland Nationals had trampled on the prerogatives of the federal parliamentary

National Party, the National Party reaffirmed that it was the prerogative of the federal parliamentary National Party to decide whether there should be a coalition. The Liberal Party made the same affirmation in relation to its own federal parliamentary party. This was a precondition to the restoration of that coalition.

In fact, the operation of the implied covenant regarding the supremacy of the party organisation on non-policy issues had done more than anything else to stop the 'Joh for PM' (later 'Joh for Canberra') campaign in its tracks. After the federal coalition had been broken, the New South Wales Nationals and New South Wales Liberals resolved that the joint Senate ticket between the two parties would stay in place for the upcoming Senate election. It went further: the New South Wales Nationals declared that if any Joh Nationals ran in New South Wales against sitting Liberals, the New South Wales Nationals would campaign for the Liberals. These two decisions destroyed any real hope the Queensland Premier had of launching his ill-conceived assault. It was formally abandoned a few weeks later.

I have not forgotten the meeting at my home in May 1987 when the leaders of the Queensland Nationals told me it was all over, and in the process poured vitriol on their New South Wales branch. Their director, the late Fred Mayberry, was especially venomous towards Doug Moppett, the New South Wales National Party President, who had led the resistance to the Queensland madness. To me, Doug Moppett was a hero.

Although the two crucial decisions taken in New South Wales were strongly supported by Nationals parliamentary leader Ian Sinclair and me, they were organisational decisions. When, early in 1989, I pushed hard to restore a joint Senate ticket in Victoria as a demonstration of unity, I knew that I could not achieve that goal unless the organisational wings of the two parties agreed. Once again, Ian Sinclair and I were strongly supportive, but we had to work hard to convince our lay colleagues. The final choice rested with a meeting of the state conference of the Victorian Nationals. Fortunately, they came on side, but it had not been a foregone conclusion.

The flexibility of the kind I have described earlier means that the Liberals more easily embrace free votes. The ALP's more authoritarian culture means that Labor MPs are accustomed to slugging it out in the caucus and then, grudgingly in some cases, getting behind the collective view and fighting the common enemy.

Free votes do not happen often, but when they do they rarely result in friction within the Liberal Party. A prime example was the vote on the republican referendum in 1999 (which I look at again in 'Long May She Reign!'). From the very beginning, I declared that Liberal senators and MPs would have a free vote. I made this known at the Constitutional Convention in 1998.

In 1999, three of the four people who comprised the leadership group of the Liberal Party – Treasurer Peter Costello, Environment Minister Robert Hill and Communications Minister Richard Alston – supported a republic and campaigned for it. I strongly supported the constitutional monarchy. Coalition senators and MPs divided approximately 70 per cent in favour of the monarchy and 30 per cent against.

By contrast, the Labor Party was a study in ambiguity. Its official policy was in favour of a republic, and this was binding on all MPs. Although I don't recall any Labor members apart from Graeme Campbell coming out for the Queen, I doubt that they all campaigned to replace her, particularly given the high number of votes recorded for the monarchy in some safe Labor seats.

It was a contrary referendum. Despite my well-known position, my electorate of Bennelong voted firmly for a republic.

Consensus of a different kind emerged in 1972 in relation to no-fault divorce. The new Labor government's Attorney-General, Lionel Murphy, and PM Gough Whitlam were both strong proponents, and there was a widespread feeling that all MPs should have a free vote on the issue. I had done some divorce work in my years of legal practice, and it was not edifying.

There was also majority support in the community for reform. Public opinion had coalesced around the notion that where a marriage had irretrievably broken down, no good purpose was served in keeping it afoot. Many traditionally conservative people, while accepting this, were concerned to ensure that the changes ushering in no-fault divorce did not result in a cavalier attitude to the institution of marriage, and that the welfare of children did not play second fiddle to the understandable desire of separating parents to be happy.

I had been an MP for under 12 months when the Family Law Bill came on for debate. A range of views existed within the Liberal Party on the Bill, but the debate revealed intense divisions within the Labor government. The ALP's more conservative members were either opposed to any major changes to the existing law, or went along with no-fault divorce provided there were safeguards to preserve the position of marriage as a bedrock social institution, and protect the welfare of children.

Among this group of members there was intense suspicion, verging on active hostility, towards Lionel Murphy, the minister responsible for carrying the legislation. Murphy epitomised the socially progressive push within the party, was openly contemptuous of the social attitudes of many of its Catholic members, and was keen to push the envelope while he had the chance. (When Lionel Murphy died in 1986, the eminent historian Manning Clark wrote that 'it had been one of Murphy's aims to dismantle the Judeo-Christian ethic of Australian society'.[1])

I encountered this hostility first-hand from the late Frank Stewart, Minister for Tourism and a devout Catholic. Typical of the cross-party approach to this issue, I worked with Stewart and Ralph Hunt, a senior National Party MP, on some amendments to the Bill. Stewart openly despised Murphy, and one night when we were working in his office, he let fly. In the process he did not spare Whitlam, who openly wanted major changes in the area of family law. Whitlam had exercised his prerogative as PM to introduce the Bill in the House of Representatives, and had done so in a dinner suit, presumably because he was on his way to a black-tie function. Stewart repeatedly sneered at this, and, given Gough Whitlam's eye for theatrics, his minister's sarcasm was understandable.

It became clear as debate on the Family Law Bill progressed that no-fault divorce would carry the day. The only issue remaining in contention was the separation period that would be accepted as demonstrating that a marriage had utterly broken down. The government's Bill provided that the period should be one year, but many felt this was not long enough.

In the end, Bob Ellicott, the Liberal MP for Wentworth, moved an amendment to increase the period to two years. The vote on this became the bellwether of the whole debate. It was defeated by the narrowest possible margin, 59 to 60. Interestingly, six past, current or future PMs voted on this amendment: Gough Whitlam, John Gorton, Bill McMahon, Malcolm Fraser, Paul Keating and John Howard. Of those six, Fraser, Keating and Howard voted for Ellicott's amendment. The other three voted against it.

Heated though the no-fault divorce debate became, the Labor Party of that era showed far more respect for individual freedom of conscience than its successor more than 40 years later. At the time of the final debates on the same-sex marriage issue in 2017, ALP senators and MPs were participating under the shadow of an explicit resolution from the party's National Conference that as of the election scheduled for late 2019, they would no longer have a free vote on the issue. They would be required to support any same-sex marriage legislation or face expulsion from the party. As it happened, the issue was fortunately resolved before this authoritarian requirement came into operation.

Currently, differences clearly exist within Liberal ranks on the issue of climate change, as I discuss in my later essay on that topic. These will continue to require careful management, but fortunately the culture of the Liberal Party is more conducive to this than the ALP's.

Worryingly, though, there are signs that the Liberal Party's flexible attitude is changing at an organisational level. State divisions in recent times have been too ready to expel or suspend members who have spoken out of turn.

As a result of factional warfare, they seem more intent on keeping people out than welcoming people in.

One example is Lyle Shelton, former director of the Australian Christian Lobby (ACL). He was a member of the Liberal National Party (LNP) in Queensland, but joined the Australian Conservatives to run as a Senate candidate in 2019. He failed, the Conservatives folded, and he applied for readmission to the Queensland LNP. He waited months for a response, lost interest and has now been chosen to replace Fred Nile in the New South Wales Legislative Council as a Christian Democrat. His values align closely with those of many Liberals. At the ACL, he echoed the views of millions of Liberal supporters on social issues.

It is true that he ran for another party. In that context I am reminded of Steele Hall, the former Liberal Premier of South Australia. After leaving that office he was instrumental in forming the Liberal Movement, at first a party within a party and later a separate party, with small-l liberal attitudes. He was elected to the Senate as a Liberal Movement man in 1974.

The Liberal Movement damaged the Liberals in South Australia a lot. When it was reintegrated into the South Australian division of the Liberal Party in 1976, Hall was readily readmitted into the federal parliamentary party room. It was the pragmatic thing to do. Hall's instincts had always been essentially those of the Liberal Party, although of a leftist variety. Yet Lyle Shelton's had been likewise, but with more of a right-wing tinge.

Even more absurd was the decision of the LNP to suspend the membership of Peter Lindsay, the former MP for the marginal seat of Herbert in North Queensland. His transgression was insignificant, involving criticism of the LNP's organisational priorities. These trends surely demonstrate the growing intensity of factionalism, which I have addressed in the preceding three essays.

Factionalism may be on the rise, but the Liberal Party has at least stayed true to its classical liberal values. When I reflect on the people who have either led the Liberal Party or heavily influenced its policy direction in the years between my prime ministership and today, there is a remarkable consistency of policy opinion on issues such as economic management and national security. There are variations in individual areas, such as levels of expenditure and of industrial relations reform. But there was complete unity behind, for example, the controversial involvement in Iraq and the introduction of the GST, as well as waterfront reform. To the extent that colleagues declared themselves, there was a range of views on the monarchy and same-sex marriage, but these issues involved free votes.

As for my own personal views, broadly speaking, I was and remain an economic liberal and a social conservative.

I support the constitutional monarchy. I voted against same-sex marriage, and I have always opposed a Bill of Rights: an issue I shall discuss in 'Constitutional Change'. Despite my belief that our treatment of Aboriginal people in the past constituted a grievous national failure, I was unwilling to embrace a formal apology to Aboriginal people. Not only did I regard the *Bringing Them Home* report, which recommended an apology, as deficient, but I also felt, as an issue of principle, that one generation cannot apologise for the alleged misdeeds of an earlier one. Only real-time apologies have credibility.

On the liberal side of the equation, my identification with economic reform is well known and has defined much of my political life. There have been successes and failures. My passionate commitment to industrial relations reform has been driven by my belief that the right of the individual to negotiate the terms of his or her own employment is greater than the right of a union to impose its version of what is good for an individual. It is respect for individual will that underpins my strong support for freedom of association. Men and women should be free to join or not join a trade union, just as they are free to worship in a church of their choice, or no church at all, or join or not join a political party, or associate with any cause that takes their individual fancy. That is the character of the society in which we live.

One of the many arguments for a GST was that it shifted, to some degree, the burden of taxation from income to consumption. We must all earn an income to survive, but we do have some discretion about what we consume. Hence a greater recognition of freedom of individual choice is inherent in a proportionately bigger impost on consumption. Government ownership of commercial organisations limits choice. Not only does it carry an implicit guarantee against failure, but it also limits competition.

These are but a few examples of where I have seen economic reform as a necessary ingredient in aligning the policies of the party with its philosophical commitment to individual freedom of choice. That has not been the only reason I have espoused such policies; I have long seen them as further strengthening our economy too. The liberation of individuals normally inspires greater personal achievement, so it is something of a circular argument.

Some people assert that there should be consistency in these things. If you are an economic liberal, almost by definition you should be a social one as well. Apart from the fact that there is no natural imperative to be so, there is an argument that economic liberalism can produce such a level of change that a society will seek stability and oppose further change in other areas of life.

From the early 1980s onwards, there was a lot of economic change, most of it beneficial. (I describe it in more detail in the next chapter.) Still, for many Australians it was personally unsettling. To them, even more change within familiar practices and institutions would have been challenging.

Although there was broad unity within the Coalition on economic policy, a solid group remained that was none too enthusiastic about too much reform, and grew profoundly sceptical of my approach of attacking the Labor government from the reformist right.

Industrial relations reform became the crucible within which a struggle emerged. There was a significant debate underway on this topic among Liberals and within the broader community. It was between those who were happy with the status quo and those who, like me, wanted major change that would break the stranglehold of the unions, and reduce the role of the Industrial Relations Commission, paving the way for individual employment contracts. The business sector was quite divided. Large manufacturing and transport companies wanted things to remain essentially as they were; small businesses, farmers and most miners wanted change.

Having seen the government float the dollar in 1983, which most Coalition MPs went along with, not all my colleagues supported my call for Bob Hawke to match that opening of the Australian economy externally with an internal liberalisation of the labour market. Not only did I believe in this, but I also knew that Labor's historical links with the unions meant that it would never occur under a Labor administration.

I was not alone in my drive for reform. There was a strong feeling among many colleagues that Malcolm Fraser had not been the reformist PM that had been expected. The sentiment was that he had wasted the huge majorities he had been given in 1975 and 1977. Now there was the further indignity that a Labor government was doing things such as floating the dollar that should have been done by the Coalition under Fraser.

Whether this was a fair judgement was not the point. That was the mood. There was a tendency for many to reject what they saw as the timidity of the past and embrace major economic reforms. After all, this was the era of Margaret Thatcher and Ronald Reagan, the centre-right heroes of the 1980s. Such achievements as Thatcher's crushing of the 1984 miners' strike and the 1986 strike by print workers at Wapping, as well as Ronald Reagan's successful confrontation of striking air-traffic controllers in 1981, warmed the hearts of many Coalition followers in Australia.

While that sentiment was strong, there was an alternative one that argued that the economic policies of Thatcher and Reagan were too right-wing, or even extremist, and quite unsuitable for Australian circumstances.

After a detailed internal debate, the issue was finally resolved in favour of reform. Neil Brown, as deputy party leader and industrial relations spokesman, released our new policy in May 1986. It had a strong deregulatory thrust, which represented a historic change for the Liberal Party. Robert Menzies had remained a staunch supporter of centralised wage fixing, often waxing lyrical about the Conciliation and Arbitration Commission (the predecessor of the Industrial Relations Commission – now the Fair Work Commission).

This new policy exemplified the victory of the individual over the collective. Effectively it ended the union monopoly on the bargaining process. Employees would be free to make their own bargains with their employers, subject to certain guaranteed conditions. Importantly, the strong Liberal principle of choice was maintained.

BIPARTISANSHIP: A ONE-WAY STREET

Reflections on balancing party loyalty with the need for economic reform

On the afternoon of 9 May 1995, I took a telephone call from Kim Beazley. He was Deputy PM as well as Finance Minister in Paul Keating's government. I had returned to the opposition leadership in January of that year. Despite our political differences, Kim and I enjoyed a good personal relationship. I had always respected his decency and intelligence. He was a dedicated Labor man who had good instincts, especially on national security issues.

Politics is a strange pursuit. Kim Beazley was removed as Labor leader because his colleagues doubted that he could defeat me in the upcoming election. Yet if he *had* remained leader, and defeated me, his colleagues would not have disposed of him in the way they did Kevin Rudd. He could have been a successful Labor PM, and if so, the politics of the past 10 to 15 years would have been very different.

But I digress. That evening the Treasurer, Ralph Willis, was due to deliver what would prove to be Labor's last budget for 12 years. Kim asked me, 'John, is it still your policy to privatise the rest of the Commonwealth Bank? Because if it is, we'll need your help to get the legislation through the Senate. The Democrats and Greens are opposed, and it will fall over if you don't vote for it. The sale proceeds are in the budget tonight.'

I responded that our policy had not changed, but naturally we wanted to see the budget and the legislation.

There had been some rumours about the possibility of such a sale, but they had been discounted because the Treasurer had given explicit assurances to the relevant unions that it would never happen. Kim's request of me was in many respects an astonishing one, and the latest in a saga of twists and turns by the Labor Party on privatisation.

For almost 10 years it had been Coalition policy to privatise government-owned business enterprises such as the bank, Telstra (then Telecom), Qantas and Australian Airlines. We had been open about it. For many years both Hawke and Keating had attacked us over our approach. Bob Hawke once described it as a 'slash and burn exercise'.[1] In his 1985 T.J. Ryan Memorial Lecture, Hawke had labelled the privatisation of the Commonwealth Bank, Qantas and

Telecom as 'socially offensive', and said that our privatisation policies were both unworkable and unwanted. They would, he asserted, cause damage to the entire community and leave ordinary Australians far worse off.

As the government's economic needs tightened, Keating as Treasurer had abandoned his previous opposition to privatisation, and sold off first Qantas and then part of the Commonwealth Bank. He had felt safe in the knowledge that the Coalition would not oppose him. He was not troubled by the rank opportunism involved.

My party did *not* oppose the sale of the remainder of the Commonwealth Bank in 1995. Not only was it critical to prevent the budget from falling over, but we would also have aped Labor's monumental hypocrisy if we had done so. On the way through, though, Shadow Treasurer Peter Costello, employing his fine rhetorical skills, inflicted some well-deserved political pain on the government by reminding Ralph Willis of the written assurances he had given the finance sector unions that what he was now begging the Coalition to facilitate would never take place.

That was only the half of it. Having turned itself inside out on the issue in government, the ALP then reverted to type by consistently opposing all attempts by the Coalition to privatise Telstra during our time in government. It was only after the Liberal and National Parties had won control of the Senate at the 2004 election that we were able to complete its full sale, with much of the proceeds being paid into the Future Fund. This sovereign wealth fund was established in 2006 principally to meet the future unfunded liabilities of retiring public servants and military personnel.

This episode was not only the apogee of the Labor Party's hypocrisy on privatisation, but also a metaphor for the Coalition's willingness to give bipartisan support on important policy issues: a gesture that was never returned when the Liberal and National Parties assumed office. In this chapter I further explore this issue in the context of some of Australia's most eventful economic reforms of recent decades.

Although never conceded at the time, there was an unspoken consensus on many areas of economic policy between the two sides of Australian politics until well into the 1970s. It would surprise most Liberal supporters now to be told that the Coalition's industrial relations policy for the 1975 election exhorted employees to join a trade union of their choice. In that same campaign, Malcolm Fraser promised that a Coalition government would 'give Australian industry the protection it needs'.[2] To those on both sides of government who had entered politics in the golden Menzies era, the prevailing order – featuring centralised wage fixation, high tariffs on imports, a regulated exchange rate and government ownership of commercial enterprises – worked. It had delivered 20 years of prosperity.

Menzies was an economic conservative, dedicated to preserving the prevailing economic order. This was because that order had delivered high living standards and social stability, and his record seven electoral victories demonstrated that it had strong public support. Between 1949 and 1972 the Australian economy grew by an average of 4.8 per cent a year: a remarkably high rate, and close to those of a developing nation during the modern era of globalisation. Inflation had averaged 4.5 per cent a year and unemployment 2 per cent. Australia's population had grown by 39 per cent. Home ownership increased from 53.4 per cent in 1947 to 68 per cent in 1971. Australia's economic engagement with Asia was effectively launched by the historic Japan–Australia commerce agreement of 1957, the same year in which the Mount Whaleback iron ore deposit was discovered in the Pilbara, paving the way for a priceless resources trade with Asia. By the mid-1970s, 100 million tonnes of iron ore were being produced in Australia.

When Gough Whitlam opened Labor's 1972 election campaign with his famous Blacktown address, he paid Menzies and his Coalition successors an unintended compliment by saying that Labor's expansive spending program could easily be paid for out of the huge automatic increases in government revenue. That campaign was, of course, conducted in the belief that the economy would continue to grow strongly, and that such strong growth would be underpinned largely by a continuation of Coalition policy.

There was no warning of the Arab oil embargo in October 1973 that produced a quadrupling of crude oil prices. Equally was the sudden change of direction by the Nixon Administration both on support for the fixed exchange-rate system established at Bretton Woods towards the end of World War II, and its flirtation with an interventionist incomes policy. Such a policy involved direct attempts by governments to control the level of prices and incomes. In addition, the US economy had been suffering from massive imbalances since the late 1960s, due to the Johnson Administration's policy of financing its social reforms and the ever-rising costs of the Vietnam War through borrowings to cover its increasingly bigger deficits.

The oil crisis, and the US policy shifts, were seismic events that shook the world economy. They would in time produce high inflation, rising interest rates and much higher unemployment in the developed world.

The Whitlam Government was unprepared for this dramatic change of circumstances. So long starved of government, this group of men felt it to be quite unjust that they should be forced to pare back any of the spending plans they had thought about for years. What Labor would later depict as the lotus years of the Menzies era were meant to have continued. So, far from applying policies that might slightly mitigate the impact of the world economic earthquake, the ALP ploughed on regardless. Strategies such as using the public service as a pacesetter when it came to wage claims only intensified the effect of what had occurred abroad. True, it wasn't Australia's fault that the world had changed so dramatically, but why make it worse?

Under Malcolm Fraser, the cross-party economic consensus remained. The Coalition's massive victory in December 1975 was not driven by fundamental differences on economic policy, beyond the argument that Whitlam had spent too much: an increase of 56 per cent in real terms in only three years of government. The Labor government had been thrown out because it was rightly deemed incompetent and unstable. The Coalition's retort was always that by spending less there would be more room for taxation reductions, which of course was correct.

Malcolm Fraser and I would have a fluctuating relationship. Yet after our party's landslide victory in 1975, he appointed me to the wide-ranging economic portfolio of Business and Consumer Affairs. It was an exciting responsibility, and I was most grateful for the confidence the newly elected PM had placed in me. After only 18 months in parliament, I had the political opportunity of a lifetime.

I was not to know it at the time, but this decision would have lasting consequences for the more than 30 years I would spend in parliament. Without Fraser's decision to make me a minister with economic responsibilities, I almost certainly would not have become Treasurer just two years later. When Malcolm Fraser put together his new ministry, many were obvious and experienced appointments, but a few slots were there for new, younger people. Despite the difficulties that would later emerge in our relationship, I have always remained grateful to Fraser for the preference he gave me then.

Expenditure control was Fraser's greatest economic achievement in his first few years of government. It was a daunting challenge, because public outlays had grown dramatically under Whitlam's undisciplined bent. But within two years, the rate of growth in government spending had been substantially cut. As my government was to learn, this is never easy.

There was much more to do, however. The old order that had obtained throughout the 1950s and 1960s was breaking down under the weight of the world economic turmoil that the Whitlam Government had been so unwilling to confront. Understandably, there was little Australia could do to escape the slipstream of these major economic events. We could, however, mitigate the consequences through some adjustment to domestic economic policy.

Yet we still lived in a Keynesian world, where fiscal policy – spending and taxation – was seen as the principal way in which governments influenced the economic cycle. The dominant view of senior members of the Coalition government was that the changed world circumstances did not require major changes to economic policy at home. They largely held that the erraticism of the Whitlam Government, particularly its big spending, had compounded the economic downturn. Change that, by continuing to bring expenditure under control, and things would right themselves.

Clear differences remained, however, on the level of expenditure required. Most of those on the centre-right argued that spending should be restrained where possible and taxation pared back, but that the government should continue to be the major actor in the management of the economy.

Significantly, though, around the world questioning of the Keynesian view had emerged, asserting that the high inflation and rising interest rates of the time were to a large degree consequences of the rapid growth of the money supply. They did not dispute the need for expenditure restraint but argued that the problems the world faced went much further. Those who held this view, loosely styled 'monetarists', drew a lot of their inspiration from Milton Friedman, the leader of the Chicago school of economists. The monetarists championed free markets, less regulation and the crucial need to reform the supply side of the economy. Yet they reached well beyond economics.

In challenging the pre-eminent place of Keynesian doctrine, the monetarists challenged the very role of government in Western liberal societies. Their philosophies were imbibed by those great conservative standard-bearers Ronald Reagan and Margaret Thatcher. In his inaugural address in January 1981, the newly elected president memorably declared that 'Government is not the solution to our problem, government is the problem.'[3]

By the time of the December 1977 election, Malcolm Fraser had a good economic story to tell: he had got the budget under control and brought inflation down. For that he deserved much credit. The government's election promises nibbled at the edges of taxation policy – for example, a pledge to abolish estate duties, which was subsequently carried out – but there were no clearly delineated debates about fundamental reform of the taxation system.

Fraser also promised at the election that if his government were returned it would establish an inquiry into Australia's financial system. This pledge owed more to the urgings of his economic advisor, Professor John Rose, and part-time Treasury advisor, John Hewson, than it did to any burning desire on the part of Fraser or the Treasury to reform Australia's financial system. Rose and Hewson were very talented economists. They felt that the Australian economy was over-regulated and in need of lasting reform. They were not alone. A growing number of commentators, including financial journalists such as Alan Wood and Max Walsh of the *Australian Financial Review*, shared their views.

Fraser was at heart an economic interventionist. While

from time to time he employed the language of the free marketeers and invoked the names of their icons, such as Milton Friedman and Ayn Rand, he never really trusted markets.

At the beginning of the 1977 election campaign, I had unexpectedly become Treasurer. Philip Lynch, who had been Treasurer, had fallen ill, and I was acting in his place when some allegations regarding land deals in which he was involved were made. He stood aside because it was impossible to satisfactorily resolve the issue in the heat of an election campaign. Fraser appointed me Treasurer in place of Lynch. After the election, Lynch was cleared of any wrongdoing in relation to the land deals.

When I became Treasurer, John Hewson seamlessly transferred to my staff and was of enormous assistance to me. The advice given to me by the Treasury was of a consistently high quality. Hewson augmented this.

I needed plenty of assistance, as it quickly became obvious that my first budget would need to be a very tough one. The tax cuts offered in the 1977 budget had been based on unrealistic fiscal assumptions. As a result, they had to be substantially taken back in the 1978 budget, and in addition there were some nasty spending reductions, all in the name of cutting the deficit.

One of my early acts as Treasurer was to fulfil Fraser's campaign promise and establish the Campbell Inquiry into

Australia's financial system. No major inquiry in recent memory has won such respect, or seen its recommendations so comprehensively implemented. Tracing its fluctuating fortunes in the hands of Australia's major political parties is a case study in commitment to lasting reform and bipartisanship, intermingled with political opportunism and cynicism. Yet the result was an open, transformed financial framework that has played a major role in the strength of our economy over the past 30 years.

Keith Campbell, CEO of the Hooker Corporation, was my choice as chairman. He impressed me as a pragmatic businessman who understood how the financial system affected everyday commerce: just the person we wanted. The other members were Alan Coates, the former boss of AMP; Keith Halkerston, a widely respected figure in the financial community; Dick McCrossin, General Manager of the Australian Resources Development Bank; Jim Mallyon, Chief Manager of the Reserve Bank; and Fred Argy of the Treasury, who acted as secretary.

The committee's work attracted great interest in the business community, and not just among those in finance. There was widespread support for a freer, less regulated financial system.

The Treasury's attitude was ambivalent. It was broadly in favour of a less regulated economy, but some of the boffins worried that too great a preoccupation with freeing the financial system would divert political eyes from the harder and less glamorous task of reining in the deficit. The Treasury's critics argued that the department was in favour of removing only the controls on the economy that were not in the Treasury's hands.

Having been enthusiastic about holding a financial-system inquiry in the first place, Malcolm Fraser became increasingly uneasy about the idea of relaxing controls. He would frequently rail against banks at cabinet meetings, and argue the case for more, not fewer, controls on financial institutions. He even raised with me the option of seeking the support of the state premiers at an upcoming meeting to impose controls on newly formed cash management trusts. These had emerged as a direct consequence of the controls on banks. I opposed the idea, and fortunately it did not proceed.

In opposing deregulation, the PM had the support of all his senior cabinet colleagues – except me.

Notwithstanding this resistance, in two areas, real progress was made. In December 1980, the Monetary Policy Committee of cabinet agreed to lift controls on interest rates paid by banks on money deposited with them. The government also introduced a tap system for the sale of Treasury bonds. In terms of economic reforms of the era, this measure was acclaimed by the former Governor of the Reserve Bank, Ian Macfarlane, in 2011 as 'second only in importance to the float of the Australian dollar in 1983'.[4] It meant that market demand would determine the interest rate on bonds issued by the government. Both decisions were consistent with what Campbell was bound to recommend. Despite his regulatory instincts, Malcolm Fraser was a strong advocate of the tap system.

Early in 1981, Campbell delivered his report. As predicted, it recommended extensive deregulation of Australia's financial system, including floating of the dollar, admission of foreign banks and the removal of controls on banks' lending and deposit rates.

At the time, the Reserve Bank set the maximum interest rate that banks could charge on housing and commercial loans of less than $100,000 (40 years ago, that was a big loan). It was an era of high interest rates, and the banks were increasingly starved of funds to service these loans. They could not offer sufficiently competitive rates, because non-bank financial institutions, which were not subject to the same interest controls, were constantly able to outbid them for funds.

To the average voter, floating the dollar was no big deal, nor was the admission of foreign banks. The local banks were unpopular. Many small businesses regarded them as stingy, and unreasonable in demanding the security of the family home even for relatively small loans. (There was a naïve belief among some that new bank entrants from abroad would bring a flood of fresh money for housing. In fact nothing could be further from the truth: they would want a share of the wholesale market and would be subject to the same interest rate realities as the existing players.)

It was the lifting of interest rate controls that concerned the public. It was far and away the most sensitive of all Campbell's proposals. There was an understandable belief in the community that if governments had controls over interest rates, they could be kept down.

Negotiating with Fraser about the terms of the government's holding response to the report was difficult. National Country Party leader Doug Anthony quickly went public with his opposition to the lifting of interest rate controls. The Labor Party opposition remained strongly against deregulation. Yet sentiment in the business community was supportive of Campbell's findings; so was much of press opinion.

During the latter stages of the Fraser Government, a growing number of senators and MPs began to stake out more free-market-driven ground. This culminated in open defiance over protection policy for the motor car industry. In December 1981, 33 senators and MPs wrote to Fraser and Phillip Lynch, now Industry Minister but still deputy leader, calling for reduced tariffs.[5] The PM and Lynch prevailed in cabinet. This was a seminal moment, as the defiance was so public and explicit.

The final three years of the Fraser Government proved frustrating for those, like me, who wanted significant economic reforms. Attempts at taxation reform, privatisation and a faster pace of financial reform were repeatedly denied. Malcolm Fraser and I fell out over the contents of the 1982 budget. Its final form was a compromise between us. It was expansionary, but not as expansionary as the Prime Minister had wanted.

Labor revelled in the policy disharmony but continued with its support for high protection. The cross-party consensus that had prevailed for so long on economic issues was beginning to fragment.

There was no indication then that in government Bob Hawke would pursue a more deregulatory approach to the financial system. When, in January 1983, I announced that the government had decided to admit up to 10 foreign banks, Paul Keating, recently appointed as shadow-treasurer, attacked the decision as having the potential to 'change by stealth the whole structure of the Australian financial sector'.[6] In February 1983 he said: 'Any logical examination of this issue leads to the inevitable conclusion that over time foreign bank entry will force up interest rates for individual borrowers, small businesses, farmers etc.'[7] Keating also asserted that the entry of foreign banks would link Australia to the instability of the international financial system and lessen federal control over domestic monetary policy.[8]

The Labor Party, led by Bob Hawke, went to the March 1983 federal election opposed to the principal recommendations of the Campbell Inquiry. Labor won a substantial majority, to sweep the Fraser Government government from power.

Fraser resigned from parliament immediately after the loss. Andrew Peacock easily defeated me for the leadership of the opposition. But foreign affairs, not economics, was Andrew's long suit. Having served as Treasurer for five years and deputy leader since April 1982, I was now able to assume greater control over the direction of Coalition economic policy than before. Yet we were in opposition, with no idea how long that would last. Having greater sway in those circumstances was cold comfort.

It was the experience of opposition that saw the differences within the Liberal Party between the so-called 'wets' and 'dries' over economic policy really take shape.

Meanwhile, there were signs that the new Hawke Government might soften its hard opposition to financial deregulation. A review committee chaired by Vic Martin, former managing director of the CBC Bank, was established to review the Campbell Report in the light of the new government's economic and social priorities.

Martin gave Campbell a big tick. His review had been a cover for the government to give itself flexibility in responding to Campbell.

Just how much the Hawke Government had shifted was revealed by its momentous decision in December 1983 to float the Australian dollar. No other economic decision in the past 40 years has had a greater long-term impact. The float was naturally accompanied by the abolition of exchange controls; these had involved obtaining government permission to send money out of the country. In one stroke, our economy was opened to the world.

Although the float's impact was immense, its implementation was simple. No legislation was required. The ordinary citizen felt no effects. The value of the dollar had always varied, only now the market replaced government officials as the judge of the competitive capacity of Australian companies.

The move substantially altered public perceptions of economic policy. Labor was seen as having outflanked the Coalition when it came to reform. The financial press was in raptures, and Keating's stocks soared – although the float had been driven by the PM and Reserve Bank Governor Bob Johnston, and Keating himself had expressed hesitation at the crucial cabinet meeting.

I supported the decision wholeheartedly, and privately mourned the fact that it had been announced by a Labor Treasurer. Speaking on the ABC's *PM* radio program that night, I described it as both 'correct and courageous'.

National Party leader Doug Anthony felt differently,

however. His private secretary Liam Bathgate had alerted me to Doug's intention to attack the float, and earlier that day, Doug and I had hotly debated the issue. Doug, for whom I had great affection, did not go ahead with his intended press statement. Not long afterwards he announced his intention to leave politics.

In many ways the floating of the dollar and my immediate endorsement of it launched a period in Australian politics when the Coalition offered bipartisan support for a series of economic decisions made by the government. In most cases, this was because the ALP had embraced *our* policies. (This was not the case with the float, however. Whereas I strongly backed it, both Malcolm Fraser and Doug Anthony had been known opponents. I assumed that Andrew Peacock went along with the float, although I don't recall any discussion with him at the time.)

I saw no point in doing anything other than supporting the government when it took decisions that I thought were economically sound. I resolved that the best method of responding to this new-look Labor approach was to argue that it should go *further* – in political terms, to attack the government from the right. It would hardly have made sense to do otherwise. Arguing *against* Keating's policies would have betrayed what I had argued over several years; it would also have caused intense disappointment to many supporters of mine, who saw me as the principal proponent of the cause of deregulation, greater economic freedom and smaller government.

It was comfortable for me to advocate reforms in which I believed, but some of these issues caused yet more division within the Liberal Party. Some of my colleagues did not favour going further than Labor in some areas. Many thought that Labor had gone too far with certain decisions, such as means-testing the aged pension.

This was a difficult one for me, as I supported the decision. The opposition decided to oppose the means test at a party meeting I was absent from, and I only learnt about it from the newspapers the following day. Correctly sensing my attitude, Bob Hawke frequently claimed that I supported his position on means-testing. All I could do, when asked, was to state the opposition's policy. To have embraced the policy personally would have been hypocritical; to have stated my real view would have hurt the Coalition.

In the 1984 election campaign, Andrew Peacock campaigned effectively against the means test. Politically he was right. It won him many votes and hurt the ALP. (Later, under my leadership, the Coalition would withdraw its opposition to the means test.)

As the months went by, Paul Keating continued to win plaudits for his handling of the economy. Under the guise of responding to the Martin Report, he progressively implemented many of Campbell's suggestions. Hawke and

Keating knew that with the departure of Fraser and Anthony, the power balance within the Liberal and National Parties had shifted towards a greater free-market disposition. Recent elections had seen the arrival of new Coalition MPs who preferred Friedman to Keynes, or at least thought that there was room for both. The PM and Treasurer felt safe in the knowledge that the Coalition would not attack policy changes that had been championed by Campbell and were consistent with the rising tide of deregulatory thinking on the centre-right side of politics.

It was only a matter of time before Keating announced that foreign banks would be allowed in. He was no longer worried about 'changes by stealth' to our financial system. Naturally I supported this change too, because it was good policy, and mimicked what I had announced in the last weeks of my time as Treasurer.

Although Labor had shifted on floating the dollar and foreign banks, it remained adamantly opposed to abolishing interest rate controls – that is, until I made it possible for the ALP to support this reform without taking any political risks.

Having won the 1984 election, the Hawke Government convened the 1985 tax summit. Keating's proposal at the summit for a 12.5 per cent consumption tax was destroyed by the unions, with Hawke's connivance. The unions had maintained their traditional opposition to any increase in the indirect tax burden. The Treasurer's strongest supporter in his attempt to broaden the tax base was me.

Shortly after the tax summit I became opposition leader. As detailed in 'Choosing the Leader', this occurred under unusual circumstances, and some believed that I had won the leadership partly because of my superior policy credentials. So there was suddenly intense interest in my policy stances, particularly relating to financial deregulation.

Naturally I reaffirmed my support for Campbell's recommendations, including removal of interest rate controls. This reform remained politically sensitive, but I had little alternative. Commentators were now applying a microscope to everything I said, and due to my close identification with the issue of financial deregulation, it was not something I could fudge. During the 1984 election Andrew Peacock had skilfully brushed the subject aside by saying it was not a priority, but without disavowing our policy. He was put under no pressure. It was quintessentially *my* issue.

As related in 'The Broad Church', one of my responses to Labor's newfound embrace of financial deregulation was to say that if the Australian economy was to be opened to the world by floating the dollar, why shouldn't it be opened internally by reforming our industrial relations system? However logical such an approach might have been, it carried many political risks, and left me exposed to opportunistic attacks from both Hawke and Keating. *They* had the political luxury of picking and choosing how far to travel down their newly selected path of economic liberalism.

Nowhere was my exposure to such attacks more apparent than in relation to the interest rate issue. They depicted me as an extreme idealogue. Despite the obvious economic fact that the existing controls were exacerbating the shortage of funds for housing at lower interest rates, the ALP persisted with the superficially plausible argument that to remove controls on lending rates would mean they rose to even higher levels. The fact that interest rates were then very high meant that their argument fell on fertile ground.

By the end of 1985, it was common knowledge that sections of the Liberal Party did not approve of the direction I was taking on economic policy. Some of the dissent was genuine; part of it was a proxy for resentment that I had become leader.

My political dilemma came to the fore in the South Australian state election in December 1985. With the aid of sections of the press, the ALP was able to make my stance on interest rates a major issue in that campaign. It was extraordinary; interest rates were not a state issue, and in any event, the South Australian Liberals had disavowed my policy of removing the controls. But that did not deter my critics. Understandably, the media were keen to exploit the growing signs of Liberal disunity, and there were rumblings that 'Howard was going too far'.

I realised that I had to blunt this attack, irrespective of its intellectual dishonesty. Early in January 1986, I announced that our policy would be modified so that the existing controls would stay on current loans but be removed on new loans. This was a sensible compromise, which in hindsight I should have embraced earlier. The average life of a housing loan was then eight years, so it would only be a matter of time before the controls went entirely.

Without any sign of blushing, Keating announced in April 1986 that the government would adopt that same approach, with nary an acknowledgement of the Coalition's stance. There was no more political juice to be squeezed from that lemon, so it was time to think of the borrowers.

It had been a long march to a rational outcome, with most of the political casualties being sustained by the Liberal Party. Yet my stance for what many had criticised as policy purity had finally made it possible to remove a huge constraint on the freer flow of money towards housing, at interest rates as low as economic conditions would allow.

There were other instances of economic cross-party support during this era. Andrew Peacock might have fiercely opposed the means test on the aged pension, but the Liberal and National Parties did not oppose the means-testing of family allowances. Budget cuts sponsored by the ALP were usually waved through in the Senate.

The end of so-called free university tuition, a holy grail of the Whitlam Government, was made possible politically by the Coalition in the 1980s when it called for the reintroduction of fees. The Hawke Government's response was the HECS scheme, established in 1989, which meant that students could delay repayment of fees for their degrees until their post-university incomes reached a certain level. It was a sensible and pragmatic way of dealing with the termination of something the nation could no longer afford. There was some hostility from student bodies, but the support of the Coalition removed all the political sting.

The examples I have canvassed contain a common theme. That is: the Coalition supported the implementation of policies proposed by Labor in government, even in cases such as privatisation where Labor had previously ridiculed the Liberal and National Parties for embracing policies the ALP had now decided to support.

Any hope that Labor would return the compliment when the Coalition won office was quickly dashed. Bipartisanship was a one-way street. Having inherited a huge deficit from the Keating Government, new Liberal treasurer Peter Costello's first budget inevitably included significant spending cuts. Labor opposed them all. Having created the fiscal hole, our opponents offered no help as we tried to fill it.

Policies we had specifically taken to the people at the 1996 election were no exception. Even our new schools policy, which facilitated the establishment of more low-fee independent schools, only made it through the Senate with the help of independent senator Brian Harradine and former Labor senator Mal Colston.

Given the organic link between the ALP and the union movement, there was no expectation on the Coalition's part that Labor would do anything but oppose all our industrial relations changes (described in 'The Broad Church'), even though they had been flagged during the 1996 campaign. The ground was well and truly marked out in this area. A full-blooded debate between the Coalition and Labor had been raging for years.

It was different with tax reform and privatisation. At various points, Labor had embraced both. In 1985 Paul Keating had been passionate about broadening the indirect tax base with his beloved 12.5 per cent consumption tax, only to repudiate that stance entirely when he campaigned successfully against John Hewson in 1993. And, as stated, having scorned privatisation throughout most of the 1980s, Labor then embraced it in the 1990s with the sale of Qantas and the Commonwealth Bank.

For some years it had been Coalition policy to fully privatise Telstra. Prior to the 1996 election we modified that approach by saying only 30 per cent would be sold and that $1 billion out of the proceeds of that sale would be invested in the establishment of a natural heritage trust. It was hoped that setting up the trust would bring an improved preference flow from green-tinged voters. None of this was to alter the ALP's voting approach. It opposed all the attempts by the Coalition government to privatise Telstra.

The same occurred with taxation reform. Our New Tax System, with the GST at its core, was unveiled on the eve of the 1998 election. Of course, the new GST was presented in all its detail, so voters knew exactly what they could expect if the Coalition were returned to office. We had not just given a general outline of the proposed reform, but had explained all the gory detail, complete with tax tables and cameos of how different individuals and groups would be affected.

That made no difference to Labor. The Coalition emerged with a clear majority in the House of Representatives, which gave it the undisputed authority to govern. Labor should have accepted that result and allowed the tax reform package through the Senate. This was not a dispute over high principle. It was a political difference, which the public had resolved in the Coalition's favour.

The passage of time has probably demonstrated that the ALP did itself a political disservice by persisting with its opposition to the GST. If it had accepted the outcome of the 1998 election and moved on to other issues, it might have been better equipped to fight the Coalition when national security emerged as the dominant preoccupation in the years that followed. Labor wrongly believed that the GST would be a 'slow burner', and wasted an entire term in opposition hoping that a major flaw in the tax package would emerge. The only occasion on which it got close was early in 2001 on petrol prices; the Coalition defused the issue by decisive action on fuel excise. By the time the 2001 election loomed, Kim Beazley's offering of a 'rollback' of the GST was seen as simply yapping at the heels of a big reform. It had become yesterday's issue.

As a postscript, the Global Financial Crisis that started in 2008 underlined again the folly of the Labor Party in not accepting the electorate's verdict of 10 years earlier. The GST understanding was to commit the net proceeds of the new tax, after elimination of the wholesale sales tax and sundry state taxes, to the states on an unconditional basis. Although reluctant to give overt praise, Labor premiers such as Peter Beattie quite liked the additional fiscal freedom this arrangement afforded them. The Global Financial Crisis reduced GST payments to the states largely because of the operation of the economic theory of elasticity of demand. For obvious reasons, demand for fresh food was largely inelastic. Demand for other items was rather more elastic. The GFC caused consumers to cut back on purchasing non-essential items, but not food. This reduced GST collections. If the GST on food had remained in the package that the Australian public originally supported, then the GST collections would not have been reduced so significantly, and all premiers, including of course the Labor ones, would have been much happier.

There is no evidence of bipartisanship in Australian politics now. Some commentators nostalgically refer to the 1980s as a golden era when the major parties came together to implement good policy. It was never as warm and cuddly as that, but I have described some of the key instances when the major parties managed to agree.

CONSTITUTIONAL CHANGE

Reflections on the delicate balances within Australian governance

The height of the COVID-19 pandemic saw an unprecedented public response from our political leaders and senior advisors. For months on end, in daily news conferences, state premiers, their health ministers and their chief health officers provided detailed updates and answered questions regarding risks, expected behaviour and progress in responding to the pandemic. There was intense public interest in these media events, largely because citizens needed to know what was being asked of them so they could plan their lives accordingly. I cannot recall a previous occasion on which state premiers enjoyed such sustained news exposure over such a long period. I suspect some of them are suffering withdrawal symptoms now that the country is finally opening up again.

It was also a time when the residents of one state were exposed repeatedly to the officials of another state; New South Wales residents would never have seen so much of the Victorian Premier, for example. Through it all, the PM and his senior ministers and health officials also featured regularly in news conferences. There was nothing different about this, particularly appearances by the PM and Treasurer. The real difference was in the intense profiles of, and focus on, the state premiers. It was the state governments, for example, that closed shops, banned crowds from attending football matches, compelled the wearing of masks on public transport and shut down schools.

In the previous 30 years there had been two other major public health campaigns, both highly successful: one to reduce the incidence of smoking and the other to combat HIV/AIDS. They were both initiated and led by the Federal Government. State governments were involved, but the Commonwealth was in the driver's seat. Both campaigns were of the public-education variety, although supporting state government action, especially the banning of smoking in government buildings, was involved. Fighting COVID-19, which required discrete intervention by government to alter daily patterns of life, was very different. For the first time in the living memory of most Australians, in order to combat the pandemic, state governments directly and extensively used powers they had always possessed but had seldom had to use. Although differences between the different states, and between the states and the Commonwealth, were highlighted, there was largely a common approach because the public health advice was essentially consistent across the country.

Assertive interventions by state governments, such as closing state borders and limiting movements, offended many Australians – although the evidence to date is that, in the majority of cases, those actions paid political dividends. The outcomes of elections in Queensland, Western Australia and Tasmania – with the incumbent governments who enthusiastically embraced restrictions soundly returned – suggest this, even if South Australia suggests the opposite. There were calls by those who objected to some of the restrictions for the Commonwealth to 'pull the states into line'. Yet the Commonwealth doesn't have the power to do so. It can argue, exhort and encourage, but not demand.

Meanwhile, the Commonwealth discharged its own responsibilities. The speedy action to close the national border, especially to China early in 2020, was crucial in preventing the spread of COVID-19. Secondly, the Commonwealth accepted responsibility for the vaccine roll-out. By far the most significant Commonwealth Government intervention was the financial rescue package in the middle of 2020, involving JobKeeper and other measures. It plunged Australia heavily into debt but saved the economy from ruin, after combined government action had effectively shut it down. It was an unprecedented level of intervention to sustain economic life, after governments had caused a recession in the name of saving lives and otherwise protecting public health.

Through the pandemic, the Australian public learnt about the structure of our federation and the respective roles of the Commonwealth and the states, which have always been there, but of which they had never really been conscious. Many Australians found themselves surprised at how significant a role has been assumed by state governments. For the past 60 years or more, financial power has accumulated in the hands of Canberra. Uniform taxation, necessitated by the exigencies of World War II, effected a huge shift in the concentration of fiscal power towards the Commonwealth.

Despite regular complaints about the centralising trend, states have shown no desire to assert their taxation independence. The public has grown used to an arrangement whereby the things taken for granted in their daily lives when they are following an agreeable pattern, such as transport to work, schooling for their children, registering a car or obtaining a driver's licence, are under the control of the relevant state government. Only such things as accessing a Medicare refund or private health insurance involve the Commonwealth, and then only tangentially and infrequently. For most citizens, most of the time, the state government is the day-to-day authority. The Federal Government is seen as having most of the power and making the big decisions that affect the whole nation.

Not surprisingly, the pandemic experience has produced debate about the respective roles of the Commonwealth and the states in our federation. There have been the usual token calls for the abolition of the states. It is a perennial in any such debate. I agree with Gough Whitlam: if we were starting Australia from scratch, we wouldn't have states; rather, we would have a strong central government and perhaps 12 or so regional governments with fewer powers than the states currently have. That is daydreaming. It's not going to happen. The Commonwealth of Australia is a federation of states, which were separately settled as colonies by the British. By a democratic process they came together to form an 'indissoluble federal commonwealth', which became Australia.[1] Any attempt to radically change the federal balance by weakening the power of the states would fail completely. For all the complaints that are made, legitimately, about the working of the federation, it has been remarkably successful. More successful, in fact, than most other democratic federations, such as the United States and Canada. Even the most passionate of nationalists among us see safety and value in a dispersal of power. I am one of them.

I remain of the view that the Australian people will never embrace radical change to the Constitution. I don't for a moment, however, reject the desirability of modest changes, not only to remedy mistakes that have existed from the beginning, but also to rectify weaknesses that have emerged along the way. To understand how we can do this, we must keep in mind the rather random distribution of those matters that can be changed by Act of Parliament and those that require constitutional change. For example, the size of the parliament (provided the House of Representatives remains double the size of the Senate) and the voting system, including the age at which people can first vote, are in the hands of the parliament. Yet the maximum term of the parliament and the procedure for resolving deadlocks between the two houses can only be altered by a referendum to amend the Constitution.

Our Constitution has both British and American antecedents. Because Australia was a federation, the writers largely copied the US federal model by giving specific powers to the national government and leaving the residue to the states. By contrast, the founding document in Canada, back in 1867, adopted a mixed approach, with particular responsibilities being respectively assigned to both levels of government. The Senate in Australia, like its counterpart in the US, is a fully elected chamber, with equality of representation by the states. The British influence was reflected in the fact that Australia fully embraced a Westminster system of parliamentary government. It is sometimes said that we copied some Swiss features as well, with our requirement that any change to the Constitution has to be ratified by a vote of the whole electorate. A majority of the Australian people have to be in favour of change, but also a majority in a majority of the six states. Our Constitution has worked well and made an impressive contribution to our enviable stability.

An unheralded virtue of our legal and political system is that we do not have a Bill of Rights. Unlike the High Court of Australia, which, as well as resolving constitutional issues, is a general appellate court of final appeal, the Supreme Court, the top judicial tribunal in the US, spends the great bulk of its time adjudicating on constitutional matters. So many of the cases it hears turn on whether a citizen's rights under the US Constitution have been violated, and inevitably the court decides issues that in Australia would be decided by the people (or the parliament). For example, the current law in the US on abortion and same-sex marriage was determined not by Congress or state legislatures, but by the US Supreme Court. In either case, the law declared by the Supreme Court was an expression of the rights of certain citizens according to the Bill of Rights. This is incomprehensible to many Australians. It certainly is to this one.

A consequence of the American situation is that controversial issues are never really resolved. Although the courts have been deciding on major social issues for more than 200 years, Americans remain restless regarding a situation where the Supreme Court can substitute its will for that of the people on issues that affect the whole community. Making decisions on disputes between companies or individuals is quite different from making a decision on an issue such as abortion.

The law on abortion is a case in point. In 1973, in the case of *Roe v Wade*, the US Supreme Court ruled in a seven-to-two judgement that a pregnant woman had the right to an abortion, because state laws limiting access to abortions represented an infringement of rights to privacy under the Constitution. Almost 50 years have now passed since that decision, but the issue remains unresolved in the minds of millions of Americans. Those who support the court's decision claim that this is an example of the unwillingness of conservatives to accept laws they don't like. There is truth in that. There is also truth in the claim that on such intensely divisive social issues, the only way to end, or at least cauterise, that division is to allow the public to decide through a democratic process what the law should be.

In the words of John Roberts, the present Chief Justice of the United States Supreme Court, when delivering his dissenting judgement in the 2015 same-sex marriage case: 'Five lawyers [the majority] have closed the debate and enacted their own vision of marriage as a matter of constitutional law. Stealing this issue from the people will for many cast a cloud over same-sex marriage, making a dramatic social change that much more difficult to accept.' He was addressing a different issue from that of abortion, but the principle applied with equal force.

I regard the wielding of such power by the courts as profoundly undemocratic, for the reason so eloquently put by John Roberts elsewhere in that same dissenting judgement: 'Whether same sex marriage is a good idea should be of no concern to us. Under the Constitution, judges have power to say what the law is, not what it should be. The people who ratified the Constitution authorized courts to exercise "neither force nor will but merely judgement".' He went on to say:

> *Understand well what this dissent is about: It is not about whether, in my judgment, the institution of marriage should be changed to include same-sex couples. It is instead about whether, in our democratic republic, that decision should rest with people acting through their elected representatives, or with five lawyers who happen to hold commissions authorizing them to resolve legal disputes according to law. The Constitution leaves no doubt about the answer.*[2]

That decision was handed down in June 2015. It is worth noting that just under seven years earlier, California, certainly a liberal state in the American sense of the term, had voted *against* same-sex marriage in a special poll.

In Australia, abortion remains controversial, but even among some of the most conservative opponents of the present law there is acceptance that, if the law were to be changed, then those who wanted change would have to make the case publicly, and thus persuade parliament to change the law. And if that were to happen, there is acceptance that public opinion would have to change. In the United States there is a deep sense of grievance that a change in the law has been imposed on the people, and against the will of the people in many states, as expressed through state legislatures. This is one of the reasons why, as I discuss in 'The Broad Church', there is such hostility to the government among many deeply patriotic Americans and therefore such a widespread refusal to participate in the democratic process at certain levels. They see it as a waste of time.

The very recent controversy arising from the possibility that the Supreme Court may overturn its earlier decision in *Roe v Wade* (by a differently constituted court) merely exacerbates the American dilemma on such sensitive social issues. In the eyes of many citizens of that country, these issues are never satisfactorily resolved when they are left to the courts. Apart from anything else they know that US presidents pay heavy regard to the personal beliefs that appointees to the court hold on such issues. That is why the Australian approach is so much better. It is also why, incidentally, the High Court of Australia is seen as politically impartial.

I am pleased that the attempt some years ago to foist a Bill of Rights onto Australia faltered. It has long been my belief that three things effectively sustain our democratic way of life. They are our robust parliamentary system, our incorruptible judiciary and our fiercely free press. We don't need a Bill of Rights. It would reduce our freedoms, not expand them.

Australians have proven reluctant to change our Constitution. Since Federation, 44 proposals to change it have been submitted to the people. Only eight have been carried. The formal burdens involved in change, and our natural conservatism, have played a role in this reluctance, as has the fact that the Constitution has worked well for our nation. It is often overlooked that it was fully approved by voters in the colonies before Federation came about. Our founding fathers were both methodical and democratic.

The law requires a full referendum in order to change the Constitution, but on certain issues a popular vote has been held where no constitutional alteration was involved. Strictly defined, these popular votes are 'plebiscites'. The most momentous of these were the two plebiscites on conscription for military service in World War I. Both were lost at the end of fiercely fought campaigns in which the ugly spectre of sectarianism emerged. As mentioned in 'Bowling Alone', differences over conscription led to the first of the three great Labor splits of the 20th century.

In 1977 the Fraser Government held a plebiscite on a replacement for 'God Save the Queen' as our official anthem. 'Advance Australia Fair' was the clear winner, gaining 43 per cent of the vote. Of the other two options, 'Waltzing Matilda' was supported by 28 per cent of voters. That was the song I voted for, and so, I think, did Malcolm Fraser. I had the rather fanciful idea that it would win, new lyrics could be written, and we would then have a really stirring national song. Monarchist though I was, I thought that by then it was high time for us to have our own distinctive anthem. 'Advance Australia Fair' was finally declared our national anthem at Bob Hawke's instigation on 19 April 1984. There was a one-word change: in the first line 'all' replaced 'sons'. It continues to be sung with gusto.

What can only be described as a poor man's plebiscite, a survey conducted by the Australian Bureau of Statistics, polled the public on same-sex marriage in 2017. Our nation had to put up with this less than adequate way of deciphering public opinion because the Labor Party and others in the Senate blocked the Coalition's measure to authorise a proper plebiscite. That was what had been promised by the Liberal and National Parties when Tony Abbott was PM. I had not supported that promise. I would have been quite happy for parliament to decide on the issue, but as the promise had been made, it should have been kept. If a proper plebiscite had been held, I am sure the result would have been the same, but we would have been spared the embarrassment of not being able to conduct a thoroughly orthodox vote on an important social issue, about which there were strongly held opposing views. It was an immature moment in our recent national story.

It is instructive that since World War II, the average voter turnout in presidential elections in the US has been 56 per cent. In the UK, the average turnout at parliamentary elections over the same period has been 73 per cent. Both countries have voluntary voting. But Britain does not have a US-style Bill of Rights. Its parliament decides major social issues, as ours does in Australia.

Philosophically, I have always been against compulsory voting, yet I never felt strongly enough to move against it when I was PM. This was partly because I had not seen evidence that the voluntary system worked much better in similar countries to ours, and because I had observed the stability in Australia that, in part at least, is a product of our compulsory approach. The Liberal Party organisation, like its Labor counterpart, was strongly opposed to any change. And, as so many are ready to point out, it is only compulsory to attend the polling booth, not to vote. After one's name is marked off, there is no compulsion to express a preference.

Emotions ran higher in the wake of the dismissal of the Whitlam Government in November 1975 than at any other time that I can recall regarding a domestic political issue. Yet despite the passion, and the venom, unleashed, the fabric of the nation held. I am sure the fact that Australians had the opportunity to vote so soon after the dramatic events accompanying the dismissal helped release the safety valve. If we had had voluntary voting, then mythology would have developed that many of those who disagreed with Kerr's dismissal of Whitlam did not bother to vote because the man they had chosen, twice, to be Prime Minister had been removed from office by the Governor-General, so what was the point?

Given the demonstrated reluctance of the Australian people to change our Constitution, the standout referendum result was surely that of 1967, which decided that Aboriginal and Torres Strait Islander people should be counted in the census, and that the Commonwealth Parliament should have concurrent power with the states to legislate for the benefit of those same people. The referendum was carried with an affirmative vote in excess of 90 per cent. There was strong bipartisan support. Although other amendments have been carried, none of them has enjoyed such a powerful endorsement.

At the same referendum, the public clearly rejected a proposal to remove the nexus clause in the Constitution, which requires the size of the House of Representatives to be as nearly as practicable double the size of the Senate. This enjoyed support from both the Coalition and the Labor Party, although it was opposed by the Democratic Labour Party. The nexus clause remains, which means that Tasmania, which has only five lower house seats because of its small population, now has 12 senators. To many (me included) the amendment proposed in the referendum made common sense. Surely an increase in the size of the House of Representatives should be possible without a parallel rise in Senate numbers. Unfortunately, the answer from the people was No.

There has been plenty of commentary over the past 50 years or more as to why the 1967 referendum on Aboriginal issues was carried so overwhelmingly. It was because it seemed eminently fair and stated the obvious. Whatever the reason why they were not included in the census count at the time of Federation, by 1967 their exclusion was seen to be monstrously wrong. Along the way the Australian people decided that the Commonwealth, as well as the states, should have the specific power to help Indigenous citizens. These changes won massive support because there was no good reason why they should not happen. They were clearly understood. Only the bigoted opposed them. The changes were not divisive. They passed the fair-go test with flying colours. The scale of the vote for these changes – over 90 per cent – was seen as a real watershed in attitudes towards the First Australians.

There is a lesson in this for the current debate about an Indigenous Voice to Parliament. The proponents of the Voice want to have a referendum to entrench it in the Constitution. There is much resistance to a constitutional change on this issue. The parliament elected on 21 May will contain 10 Indigenous senators and MPs, which will be above their proportion of our total population. This will strengthen opposition to a separate clause to enshrine the Voice. Even those who support the broad concept say the Voice should first be put in legislation, and only proposed as an addition to the Constitution if proven to be effective and non-divisive. However, most Aboriginal leaders, including Noel Pearson, reject this. They want it placed directly in the Constitution. In my view, the lessons from the 1967 referendum should be followed. On that occasion the Australian people voted resoundingly for something that was simple, and to which no fair-minded Australian could reasonably object. On the information available to date, the Voice may not fit those criteria.

When Aboriginal and Torres Strait Islander leaders produced the Uluru Statement from the Heart, one of them, Noel Pearson, was dismissive of any change to the Constitution that would merely be empty symbolism. I could be wrong, but presumably an acknowledgement that Aboriginal and Torres Strait Islander people were here before anyone else would be seen as tokenism. Yet that is a superficial judgement. Many among the millions who voted Yes in 1967 were ashamed that Indigenous people had been seen as being of so little account when the Commonwealth was formed in 1901 that it had not been thought necessary to count them as part of the Australian population. Equally, why wouldn't millions of Australians now think it the most natural thing in the world to acknowledge in our founding document that the First Australians were here before anyone else? It would be stating a simple truth. It would not be divisive. For a nation that takes pride in the fact that Australia's population comes from the four corners of the earth, it would pass as strange for such a constitutional addition to be rejected. Yet, given the opportunity in 1999 to do precisely that, the Australian people rejected it.

Remembering the famous injunction that context is everything, the circumstances of that rejection should be recalled. The day of 9 November 1999 was the one on which the Australian people, by a margin of 55 per cent to 45 per cent, voted against our nation's becoming a republic. (I shall return to this referendum in 'Long May She Reign!') They also rejected, by a greater margin, the insertion into the Constitution of a preamble that, inter alia, would have honoured 'Aborigines and Torres Strait Islanders, the nation's first people, for their deep kinship with their lands and for their ancient and continuing cultures which enrich the life of our country'. The preamble had initially been drafted by that great Australian poet the late Les Murray. There were other statements in the proposed preamble honouring features of our history and those who had made a special contribution to it, as well as the values common to most of us.

Many who voted against the preamble agreed with its sentiments but were totally focused on the proposal for a republic. To them the preamble was a diversion. My recollection is that there was very little focus on the preamble during the referendum campaign. If the preamble had been a standalone proposal, the outcome could well have been different.

I would like the words quoted above (or words to a similar effect) included in our Constitution. That would need a referendum. Unless I am very much mistaken, a proposal along the lines of what I support, if put to a referendum, would enjoy a similar level of support to that afforded to the 1967 proposals. As things stand at present, however, there is little prospect of such a vote.

As for the Indigenous Voice to Parliament, I will determine my view on it when the Albanese Government tells the Australian public precisely what it has in mind. My suspicion is that anything that carries the taint of divisiveness will fail as a referendum question.

It will be obvious from what I have written so far that I do not believe that the Australian people will vote for major changes to our Constitution, even if they enjoy bipartisan support. On such issues we are a conservative lot, and with good reason. The stability and prosperity that we see all around us, and which is such a magnet to millions from around the world, is not only something we cherish, but is also almost daily reinforced by the adverse experiences of others, even those in countries we see as close to us and friendly. Here I think especially of the huge death tolls in the United States and Great Britain, compared with Australia, during the COVID-19 pandemic.

This does not mean that debate will not continue about significant constitutional change. Nor should it preclude discussion about less ambitious, but more achievable, change.

In 2003, I raised the desirability of an amendment to section 57 of the Constitution, known as the deadlock provision, which provides for a double dissolution of both houses of parliament if the Senate, within an interval of three months, twice rejects a substantially similar Bill passed by the House of Representatives. A reconstituted parliament after the double-dissolution election can then hold a joint sitting of the two houses that will have the power to pass the rejected Bills. Such a joint sitting has only been held once in federal history, after the 1974 election which, incidentally, brought me into parliament.

The amendment I wanted made was to eliminate the double-dissolution election as a precondition to the holding of a joint sitting. The present section 57 can act as an enormous constraint on a government that has obtained a clear mandate for a major but contested reform. The classic example in modern times was the GST. The entire reform package had been submitted to the electorate in the 1998 election and, despite a heavy loss of seats, the Coalition emerged with a comfortable majority in the lower house. The public had returned the government in full knowledge that it planned to implement a new tax system. There were no vague generalisations before the election. The impact was laid bare in almost stupefying detail. As is well known, the non-government parties and independents remained in control of the Senate, and it was only possible to secure passage of the GST legislation by agreeing to certain amendments sought by the Australian Democrats.

The outcome, the GST we now have, was a historic reform that greatly improved our tax system, but it could have been even better. Indeed, it could have been the GST the Australian public supported at the ballot box in 1998. The alternative to striking a deal with the Democrats would have been to present the legislation to the Senate twice, see it rejected, and call a double dissolution of parliament. The latter would have been absurd: not only politically reckless and very likely fatal, but also utterly confusing to the public.

The nation had just been through an election largely fought over the GST, following months of debate over tax reform, and had grown weary with the subject. Many would have concluded that being dragged back to the polls again on the same issue was a sign of government incompetence, not policy determination. A third alternative, of course, would have been to abandon the whole tax plan. That would have been abject political surrender. It would have destroyed any prospect of meaningful tax reform for a generation and condemned the Coalition to near-certain defeat at the next election.

If the amended section 57 had been in place, then it would have been possible to have carried the taxation plan endorsed by the public at a joint sitting. After the 1998 election, the Coalition had a majority of 12 in the House of Representatives. The combined non-government vote in the Senate was 41. The government had 35 senators. It would have been tight, but the Coalition would have prevailed and carried the day by six votes.

In case anyone might think that such a change would have conferred a significant and unfair advantage on earlier Coalition governments, I point out that the Morrison Government would not have had a majority at a joint sitting, nor would have the Turnbull Government elected in 2016. The Abbott Government would have, but not the Gillard Government, which, with the help of independents, governed after the 2010 election. Kevin Rudd's government, elected in 2007, would have had a majority. My fourth government had control of both houses. My first, second and third governments would have had a majority at any joint sitting under the dispensation being discussed. It would not in any way pervert the political wishes of the Australian public but might embolden both sides of the parliament to attempt more courageous reforms. That would be an unalloyed benefit for the Australian public.

As a footnote to this analysis, lest it be thought that it is self-serving to base the case for change on my own experience with the GST, Kevin Rudd could have been a major beneficiary of such a constitutional provision. His climate change policies were a big reason why he won in 2007. His government's proposals for an emissions trading scheme were opposed from both directions, by the Coalition and the Greens. In a classic case where the perfect became the enemy of the good, the Greens combined with the Liberal and National Parties in the Senate to defeat the Rudd plan, because for the Greens it did not go far enough. The nation was denied an emissions trading scheme, something it had clearly voted for in 2007. It had also been part of the Coalition's manifesto for that poll, albeit in a different form. A joint sitting in accordance with the approach contemplated in my projected amendment would have seen the ALP's vote easily exceed the combined votes of the Coalition, Greens and others, because of the Labor Party's comfortable majority in the lower house. I did not agree with Kevin Rudd on climate change, but that is not the point. The paralysis that we have experienced on this issue over the past decade might have been avoided but for the rigidities of the present section 57 of our Constitution.

A change such as this requires bipartisan support, but that seems unlikely soon. There was little enthusiasm for it when raised by me, and again when the idea was briefly revived by Tony Abbott at least a decade later. It should remain on the table. When our Constitution was written, the intention was that the Senate would be a states' house. For a long time now it has reflected the partisan divide of the House of Representatives. The present wording of Section 57 reflects the original intention for the Senate. Difficult though it may appear to obtain bipartisan agreement on a suitable amendment, it is clearly desirable to provide a more balanced way of resolving deadlocks between the two houses.

CLIMATE CHANGE AND NUCLEAR POWER

Reflections on balancing climate change alarmism and economic reality

I remain an agnostic on climate change. I also believe that nuclear power should be an integral part of any energy future that relies less heavily on fossil fuels.

There is strong evidence that the earth's climate has warmed from identifiable dates during the past several hundred years, and that much of that has been due to the increased emission of greenhouse gases. Clearly human activity, particularly that involving the use of fossil fuels, such as coal, oil and gas, has contributed to those greater emissions. Debate continues about the proportionate causes of the rise in greenhouse emissions. How much is human-induced and how much is due to natural causes? Allied to this is debate about whether the change is linear or cyclical.

The world has passed through cold and warm periods in the past.

The bulk of world scientific and political opinion holds that mankind must move as quickly as possible away from the use of fossil fuels to the use of renewable energy sources such as wind and solar. There is a doomsday character about much of the debate. If the more alarmist predictions are to be believed, then within less than 100 years our planet will be far less accommodating to life as we now know it.

I am not blind to the scientific arguments, but neither can I ignore the almost religious fervour with which the climate change argument has been embraced by many, and the absurdity of some of the symbolism. The apotheosis of this was surely when a 16-year-old Swedish girl appeared on the front cover of *Time* magazine as the person of the year. But then, *Time* was the publication that, on 24 June 1974, warned that a new ice age was in prospect:

> *However widely the weather varies from place to place and time to time, when meteorologists take an average of temperatures around the globe they find that the atmosphere has been growing gradually cooler for the past three decades. The trend shows no indication of reversing. Climatological Cassandras are becoming increasingly apprehensive, for the*

weather aberrations they are studying may be the harbinger of another ice age.[1]

Apocalyptic warnings have been wrong in the past. Who can forget the dire predictions of the Club of Rome – a body formed in the late 1960s composed of former diplomats, as well as scientists and philanthropists – contained in its 1972 publication *Limits to Growth*? Members believed that unless there was less consumption of resources, the world would face a crisis. They were proved wrong. Population growth has been slowing since the late 1960s, food supply has not collapsed and, importantly, the economic growth of the past four decades has lifted hundreds of millions out of poverty. As 'The China Dilemma' will argue, the economic growth of China has played a large part in that. Such growth would not have been possible without the use of fossil fuels. Is it any wonder that the Chinese are unwilling to surrender that use without an affordable and reliable replacement?

Most media outlets have signed up to the warnings of disaster. Every extreme weather event is almost invariably attributed to climate change. Yet a sober assessment of the facts suggests otherwise. Bjørn Lomborg, president of think tank the Copenhagen Consensus Center and a courageous challenger of shrill climate-change alarmism, has called out the presentation of recent forest fires in the US as having been caused by climate change. Writing in *The Australian* on 11 September 2021, he said:

> *... this year's burned area to date is the seventh lowest of the past 20 years. Last year, 11 per cent of the annual area burned compared with the early 1900s. Contrary to climate cliches, globally burned area has declined dramatically since 1900 and continues to fall through the satellite area.*[2]

Lomborg also drew attention to a study published in the esteemed medical journal *The Lancet* that reported that temperature rises during the past two decades in Canada and the US had meant more than 7200 heat deaths a year from that warming. The *Lancet* study also showed that the warming reduced cold deaths over the same period by 21,000.[3] Surely both statistics are relevant.

Al Gore, the former US Vice President, is a leading proponent of action to reduce greenhouse gas emissions. In 2013 he stated on the ABC's flagship current affairs program *7.30* that there was a clear link between climate change and a spate of bushfires then raging in eastern Australia. By a remarkable coincidence, the following evening, the ABC presented an excellent series on art in Australia that focused on the iconic painting by William Strutt called *Black Thursday*. It depicted a huge bushfire in Victoria that burnt out one-quarter of the land mass of that state, destroyed 1 million sheep and killed 12 people. Press reports at the time said that the fire was so intense that embers fell onto a ship 20 miles out to sea. That fire occurred in 1851, during a time when the world was not experiencing any global warming. The art program was inconvenient timing for both Mr Gore and others who employed his arguments.

The climate alarmists have never been reluctant to argue that the world will suffer irreversible economic damage if we do not act promptly to counter climate change. In 2007, British Prime Minister Tony Blair and his soon-to-be successor, Gordon Brown, rolled out Sir Nicholas Stern, a senior British Treasury figure, to report on the economic consequences of not acting on climate change. Stern's report was dripping with catastrophic warnings. His core argument was that immediate and quite drastic action to reduce greenhouse gas emissions would deliver a stronger economy in decades to come. The Stern Report was embraced by the British Labour government and the Conservative opposition, whose new leader, David Cameron, had replaced the party's old torch emblem with a green tree branch, to signify its modernisation and green credentials. The ALP opposition in Australia also bowed before Stern. Overall, the report added to the climate-concern momentum of the time.

The reception first extended to Stern's report abated somewhat when it came under heavy attack for its claimed economic flaws. Writing in the *Yale Economic Review*, the eminent economist William Nordhaus, a Nobel laureate, attacked the near zero-time discount rate employed by Stern in his report.[4] In the *Review* of May 2007, he said that such a discount rate was incompatible with real-world interest and savings rates. This meant that Stern had not allowed sufficiently for future changes in interest and savings rates. The validity of that discount rate was crucial to the economic forecasts made by Stern. Nordhaus's professional specialty is the economic consequences of climate change; he is no climate-change sceptic but has cast doubt on the feasibility of the Paris target of 2 per cent reduction in greenhouse gas emissions set in 2015.

Nigel Lawson, Chancellor of the Exchequer in the Thatcher Government, made the same criticism of Stern in his book *An Appeal to Reason.*[5] Lawson also pleaded for a sense of proportion. He made the powerful point that the present generation should not carry too heavy a burden so that future generations are only 8.5 times wealthier rather than 9.5 times. This highly relevant observation was made in the context of an estimate by the Intergovernmental Panel on Climate Change – the chief UN body putting the scientific case for action on climate change – that global GDP per capita would increase 14-fold over the century, and that in the developing world the increase would be 24-fold. These analyses damaged the Stern Report in the eyes of some, but the growing army of concerned citizens was largely oblivious.

I was always conscious that the gathering world consensus on how to deal with global warming – as it was once more accurately called – posed greater challenges to Australia than it did to many other advanced countries. Possessed of vast quantities of high-grade coal, iron ore and natural gas, as well as deposits of easily recoverable uranium ore that account for 38 per cent of the world's supply, Australia was, and remains, a net exporter of energy. That made us quite different from many other wealthy developed nations. Australia's fossil fuel resources also underpinned the availability of much relatively cheap energy, especially electricity, which had been so critical to our economic growth.

It would repeatedly amaze me how ready many enthusiasts for action on climate change were to cast aside that huge advantage Australia had in the name of joining an international consensus. Australia was being asked by other affluent nations to give up an advantage those countries would not have been willing to forgo. European nations occupied the ground floor of the international rule-making process.

More than a little self-interest attended the initial choice of 1990 as the base 'business as usual' starting point to measure reductions in greenhouse gas emissions. I became acutely conscious of this on my first visit to Britain after becoming PM. This was in July 1997, only weeks after Tony Blair had entered Downing Street. Blair, whom I liked a lot, and who would be my British opposite number for the whole time he was PM, shared none of my agnosticism on climate change. In our principal meeting he sang lustily from the European hymn sheet. He declared that Europe could meet any targets set by international gatherings, and that they were desirable in the long-term interests of the world.

What neither he nor other European leaders acknowledged openly was that the de-industrialisation of East Germany, and to a lesser extent other parts of the old Eastern Bloc, following the communist implosion in 1989 to 1991 had fortuitously delivered a major reduction in projected greenhouse gas emissions. Closer to home, Blair also pointed enthusiastically to the greenhouse dividend from the closure of many uneconomic British coal mines over previous years. Both developments represented money in the bank for Europeans at any international climate negotiations, and without the antecedent pain of imposing policy change designed to deliver that dividend.

Quite by chance, I had watched the movie *Brassed Off* on the flight to London. It was a rather touching tale of a colliery band from a poor community in the North of England that had won a competition, the finale of which was at the Royal Albert Hall in London. The underlying theme of the movie was how heartless it had been of the Thatcher Government to have allowed uneconomic coal mines to close. When accepting the trophy at the Royal Albert, the band leader delivered a broadside against the Iron Lady. Of course, those pit closures had been vigorously opposed by Tony Blair's British Labour Party. I didn't mention the movie to Blair.

Australia signed up to the Kyoto Protocol in 1997, after Environment Minister Robert Hill did an excellent job by, among other things, securing acceptance of land-clearing practices in calculating the growth of greenhouse gas emissions. I never supported ratification of the protocol, because the treaty itself did not include the United States (which was opposed to ratification under both Democrat and Republican administrations) or developing countries. If we had ratified, then, for example, a company wanting to build a smelter in Australia would find it more economical to build it in Indonesia, because the obligations assumed by Australia after ratification would not apply if it were built in Indonesia, a country not bound by Kyoto. There would be no fewer emissions from an Indonesian-based smelter, and the net loser would be Australia. It seemed a clear case of protecting the national interest.

In 2001 my government dipped its toe into the water of renewable energy targets, by requiring energy producers to source 2 per cent of their supply from renewable sources.

Three years later, we rejected a recommendation from the Tambling Inquiry to move to 20 per cent. That ultimately happened under the Rudd Government.

It was a mistake for the Coalition opposition to support this generous subsidy for renewables. In 2014, the Warburton Inquiry, established by the Abbott Government to examine the renewable energy scheme, would conclude that the scheme was an expensive emissions abatement tool and provided an economically inefficient subsidy. The inquiry recommended, in vain, that the targets be rolled back. The subsidy remains a major market distortion. There should be little wonder that investment was attracted to wind and solar.

The government's White Paper on Energy, released in 2005, had spelt out the Coalition's philosophy on energy and climate change, which reaffirmed the central role of cheap, reliable sources of energy in Australia's economic future. Excise and other tax treatments of fuel were rationalised, any increase in the renewable energy target was rejected, and there was heavy emphasis on encouraging new technologies designed to reduce emissions from fossil fuel use. This included a new $500 million fund, established to encourage investment in such technologies. There was also a solar cities program, and nuclear power was certainly not given the cold shoulder. The big message was the encouragement of technological ways of cutting greenhouse gas emissions, such as through carbon abatement or storage. While an emissions trading scheme was not totally rejected, the white paper was lukewarm about it because of the absence of likely global action on that front.

It was only a matter of time before nuclear power bubbled back to the surface as an alternative power source option. Australia was happily exporting its uranium to many nations, including Russia and China. In 1998 the Howard Government had not opposed the current prohibition on a nuclear industry in Australia as a trade-off with the Democrats and Greens in the Senate to secure passage of legislation to maintain the nuclear medical facility at Lucas Heights in Sydney. The prohibition was inserted as an amendment to the main legislation. With the benefit of hindsight that was mistaken, but the immediate reason was clearly in the public interest. Labor opposed the measure to maintain the facility, so without Green and Democrat support it would have failed.

Nuclear power is emissions-free. In 2006 the Chief Scientist confirmed in writing that the only dependable sources of baseload power were fossil fuels and nuclear energy. Yet Australia seemed frozen on the nuclear issue, notwithstanding that many European nations relied quite heavily on it. France drew something like 80 per cent of its electricity from nuclear power. A previous ALP government had banned uranium sales to India, but on my visit there in 2006, I agreed with my Indian counterpart that this prohibition should be lifted. Kevin Rudd supported a similar position in 2008. As PM, Julia Gillard started talks about lifting the ban in 2011, and the final agreement to do so was signed by Tony Abbott in 2014.

The nuclear disarmament sentiment had always been strong in Australia. I recall the Palm Sunday marches of the early 1980s, which attracted the participation of groups across the political spectrum. In common with other societies, Australians have harboured a dread of a nuclear holocaust. The passage of time has nonetheless encouraged the belief that the peaceful use of nuclear energy is compatible with the pursuit of a grand bargain between the superpowers to eliminate nuclear weapons.

Every so often, an accident, such as that in 1979 at Three Mile Island in the US, would shake confidence in the peaceful industry. Seven years after Three Mile Island, the appalling Chernobyl accident, which revealed sloppy and negligent practices in Russia, seriously undermined the belief of many that the peaceful use of nuclear could ever be safe. The 2011 Fukushima accident in Japan, which had experienced the dropping of atomic bombs on Hiroshima and Nagasaki in 1945, had a particularly chilling effect on Australia. Yet the end of the Cold War had altered international attitudes towards nuclear power. Although the number of weapons remained high, the petering out of great-power rivalry gave mankind pause to hope that the world was now safer. Years later, the rise of international terrorism provided the new fear that nuclear weapons would fall into the hands of some of the practitioners of that evil art.

Yet, almost inevitably, a debate about using nuclear power had gathered pace in Australia, and this was evident while I was still in office. I didn't need the Chief Scientist to tell me that nuclear and fossil fuels were the only reliable power sources, although it helped that he did. I wanted to attract attention to the nuclear option. So, in mid-2006, I asked Ziggy Switkowski, a physicist before he entered the world of business (and head of Telstra when it transitioned to a private company in the early 2000s), to lead a group to report on the feasibility of a nuclear power industry. The group found that, with appropriate legal changes and financial help at the start, a nuclear power industry was feasible. It would in time be quite competitive with renewables and free of emissions. If a start were made in 2020, there might be 25 plants in operation by 2050, providing approximately one-third of our electricity needs. Switkowski found that, since two of the accidents mentioned above, the industry had greatly improved operating procedures, which had made production of nuclear energy more efficient and meant that less radioactive waste was produced. The report also concluded that waste disposal could be safely and effectively handled in Australia because of its geological formations.

Reactions when the report came out in late 2006 were predictable. Kim Beazley, still ALP leader, opposed a nuclear industry and said the next election would be a referendum on nuclear power. There was nervousness all round. Malcolm Turnbull, then Environment Minister, said there would be no plant in his electorate. So did Russell Broadbent, a Victorian Liberal MP. It remained a sensitive issue, but I knew that if we were returned at the upcoming election, nuclear power would attract growing attention. In a world in which fossil fuels received increased opprobrium, in which the public was becoming increasingly seduced by climate alarmism, and in which nuclear power was greenhouse-free, that was natural. The election loss in 2007 meant that I did not have to face the issue in government.

Fifteen years later, the fundamentals in the debate have intensified. Fossil fuels are increasingly under siege in the developed world. Many financial corporations, including major Australian banks, have joined the climate consensus by actively discriminating against coal. Renewables, courtesy of continued subsidies, remain competitive, yet no sustained answer to the sun's failure to shine and the wind's failure to blow has yet been found.

Many of those clamouring for the rapid phasing out of coal remain selfishly indifferent to the predicament of, for example, low-income citizens of India who desperately need affordable electricity in their homes and schools.

That is precisely the need that coal from the Adani mine in Queensland will meet. These services are staples of the frugal middle-class life we took for granted decades ago. Those who condemn China and India for continuing to rely so heavily on coal-fired power stations should remember that the electricity they produce is their people's passport to a better standard of living. If the developed world had a completely reliable renewable substitute, the Paris Agreement might have two more signatories.

The sudden vulnerability of some European nations to supplies of energy from Russia, following the sanctions imposed on that country in response to Russia's appalling attack on Ukraine in February 2022, highlights the absurdity of pressure to accelerate the phasing out of fossil fuel use. Within just a few weeks, the world energy scene became uncertain. There has been a scramble in Europe to replace fuel previously obtained from Russia. Germany has radically changed its approach. Many now question the wisdom of an earlier decision by that country to turn away from nuclear power. The fossil fuel assets of countries such as Australia could well be in even greater demand. What we do know is that the confident predictions of the climate alarmists, just a short time ago, have been placed in serious doubt because of the volatility of energy supplies from Russia.

The international consensus as I write is that, if catastrophic damage is to be prevented, global warming should be limited to 1.5 degrees Celsius above pre-industrial levels by the turn of the century. This is even more ambitious than the target of 2 degrees Celsius that underpins the Paris Agreement. To achieve this, carbon dioxide emissions must fall to near zero only by 2050.

Nuclear power is a low-carbon source of energy. As recently as 2018, it produced about 10 per cent of the world's electricity. Along with other energy developments, including expanding renewables and switching from coal to gas, higher nuclear-power production contributed to the levelling of global carbon dioxide emissions in 2019. Putting to one side the generic arguments about the threat posed by climate change, it can scarcely be argued that Australia should not concern itself with the place of nuclear power in its own and the world's energy future. Our huge reserves of low-cost uranium alone demand it.

Quite legitimately, those in our community who ring the alarm bells the loudest about climate change invariably invoke science to silence any perceived dissenters. Yet when it comes to the use of nuclear power, the view of many scientists that nuclear power must be part of the response to the climate challenge is frequently ignored. When it comes to pronouncements about nuclear power, apparently it is in order to ignore the science.

Public opinion is more fluid. While it ebbed, flowed and then hardened against nuclear energy in the wake

CLIMATE CHANGE AND NUCLEAR POWER

of Fukushima, in 2019 a Morgan Poll showed that 51 per cent of Australians supported the development of nuclear power to reduce carbon dioxide emissions. The poll also showed a large increase of 16 per cent in favour of nuclear power since a similar poll in 2011. Without the reference to reducing emissions in the questions, the support level fell to 45 per cent, still ahead of those who are opposed to using nuclear power. Nevertheless, if the government were to embrace nuclear energy as part of its climate-change response, the path would be difficult, particularly obtaining passage of legislation through the Senate to repeal the 1999 Act that prohibits an Australian nuclear industry. Labor's formal position remains opposed, but influential sections of the union movement show signs of supporting a nuclear industry. For many traditional ALP supporters, there would be the attraction of new jobs in the developing industry.

The recently announced AUKUS agreement between Australia, the US and Britain for Australia to acquire nuclear-powered submarines has been widely welcomed. That is a clear sign that public opinion has shifted. The present Labor leader and Prime Minister, Anthony Albanese, would not find it easy to repudiate the opposition he has fiercely voiced in the past. Naturally the Greens would be strongly opposed. The combined Labor–Green vote in the Senate after the May election is 38, precisely half the chamber.

No discussion about climate change would be complete without mentioning an emissions trading scheme. Back in 2006, consistent with the gathering consensus around climate change, the Business Council of Australia, representing large companies, argued for a nationwide emissions trading scheme, partly to head off the development of schemes at a state level. Late in that year, I appointed a task group of senior public servants and business figures to report on how such a scheme might work. Chaired by Peter Shergold, the head of my department, it was the gold standard in government–business cooperation. Treasury Secretary Ken Henry, Industry Secretary David Borthwick and head of DFAT Michael L'Estrange, represented the public service. Included from the private sector were Margaret Jackson, the Chairman of Qantas, Peter Coates, the boss of Santos, and John Stewart, the CEO of the National Australia Bank. The group worked well and produced its report by the required date of 31 May 2007. It recommended the introduction of a cap-and-trade emissions trading system as soon as practicable. This is 'an emissions trading regime in which a limit (or cap) is placed on the total emissions allowable from the activities or sectors covered under the scheme. Emissions limits are set below what they would be under a "business as usual" scenario'.[6] The government accepted the recommendations with few caveats.

There was a broad understanding that Australia's implementation of this new system was dependent on whether other countries did likewise, although not enough was said at the time to make this clear. Seamless though the process appeared, there was an element of box-ticking about what my government had done. We were not seen as emotionally on board with the cause at a time when the idea of being seen to be doing something about climate change had captured the public imagination, especially among the young.

The truth was that the Coalition was composed of people who shared a full range of opinions on the issue, from total sceptics such as Finance Minister Nick Minchin, to others who were in every way true believers. There was quite a strong commitment to supporting technological solutions, which was one of the reasons why we enthusiastically joined the Asia-Pacific Partnership on Clean Development and Climate, along with the US, China, India, Japan and Korea. Canada joined some time later. The main goal of the group, which between its members accounted for more than 50 per cent of the world's emissions, was to accelerate the development and deployment of clean energy technologies. There was no mandatory enforcement mechanism, which drew criticism from proponents of the Kyoto approach, but importantly, both China and India were participants. Australia would later sign a separate agreement with China on clean coal technology.

Significantly, technology was at the heart of the plan that Scott Morrison took to the UN Climate Change Conference in Glasgow in November 2021, as it had been the essence of the Energy White Paper of 2005. That was barely surprising. Throughout history, technology has provided the basis for measurable increases in living standards. That is why the Chinese and Indians cling to the energy sources they know will continue to underpin their industrialisation.

Those who draw their policy anchorage from market principles continue to be conflicted by the recognition of the role played by cheap accessible fossil fuels in Australia's economic superiority, and by their concern that the weight of public opinion will ultimately force change, and such change may not be very obedient to those market principles. Continued subsidies for renewables are evidence of this.

The climate change issue has bedevilled the Coalition since I left politics, but it would be an over-simplification to characterise the differences as reflective of a divide between conservatives and classical liberals. It is not as if some Liberal MPs are totally rejecting the need to contain the growth of greenhouse gas emissions. In any event, they are not saying so. The argument is about the pace of change, and the place of fossil fuels in the transition to renewables.

Increasingly, also, it will be about the role of nuclear power in the energy world of the future.

LONG MAY SHE REIGN!

Reflections on the balance within
Australia's constitutional monarchy

As I write, we are just several months into the Platinum Jubilee year of the reign of Queen Elizabeth II. This indomitable lady has surpassed all others in both the length and consistency of her service. Something approaching 85 per cent of Australians now alive have known no other monarch.

I was 12 years old when she succeeded her father at the age of 26. Joseph Stalin then remained the murderous dictator of the Soviet Union. The pain and suffering of World War II still hung over our lives. The Cold War had been underway for just a few years. Australian troops were fighting under the United Nations flag in South Korea. Australia had begun the great migration experience that would strengthen our nation and give hope and comfort to so many in search of a new life.

The Queen's coronation in June 1953 and her visit to Australia early in 1954 are vividly recalled by all who lived through them. She and her husband the Duke of Edinburgh were young, energetic and dedicated. In a rather romantic fashion, there was talk of a new 'Elizabethan age'. Yet for all the euphoria, most Australians accepted that the new queen faced a vastly different world from the one that had confronted her father when he became King in 1937.

The United States had emerged from World War II as the dominant victor. The addition of that country's size, wealth and industrial might had made victory possible against both Germany and Japan. The Russian people had paid a terrible price in blood and treasure: 28 million of its soldiers and citizens had perished in the German onslaught. The war had left Britain spent and exhausted, compounding the ongoing human and economic consequences of the previous world war. Yet history will forever record that for more than a year after the fall of France and other European countries, the United Kingdom, supported by its close Commonwealth allies such as Australia, stood alone against the Nazi juggernaut. Without that stoicism, ultimate victory would not have been achieved.

The fall of Singapore, arguably the most humiliating British defeat in either of the two world wars, left Australia potentially exposed to Japanese invasion. Decisive American naval victories at Midway and the Coral Sea turned the tide, and the judgement emerged that Australia had been saved by America.

The Soviets never retreated from their conquests as they rolled the Germans back. The Nazi surrender left Moscow physically in charge of most territory east of Germany, including what would soon become East Germany. Communist diktat was imposed and Europe, and by extension the world, divided into two camps. One, led by the US, was democratic, and the other, led by the Soviet Union, was communist dictatorial. Their demarcation was the Iron Curtain, memorably invoked by Winston Churchill in his speech at Fulton, Missouri, in 1946. So had begun the Cold War.

The events of World War II had ended the belief that Britain was Australia's ultimate security guarantor. The ANZUS Treaty, signed by the US, Australia and New Zealand in 1951, was eloquent testament to this. Relations between Australia and Britain nonetheless remained intimate. The ties of history, language and culture were deep and abiding.

The continuation of the monarchy as part of Australia's constitutional structure was never seriously questioned, except by a small minority of dedicated republicans – that was, until 1975. Whatever the merits or otherwise of the dismissal of Gough Whitlam, it involved the termination of the commission of an elected PM by the Queen's representative. It has been established, almost to the point of exhaustion, that the Queen herself remained studiously aloof from the constitutional wrestle that culminated in Whitlam's removal, and that it instead involved the exercise of powers completely vouchsafed to the Governor-General – an Australian appointed to that role on the recommendation of Gough Whitlam himself – by the Australian Constitution. Yet it inevitably ushered in debate about the monarchy, as the dastardly deed had been done by 'the Queen's man'.

When Bob Hawke became PM in 1983 the most he would do was declare 'Advance Australia Fair' as our national anthem: a long overdue move. He baulked at any change to our flag. Alive to the popularity of the Queen, when pressed on the issue, he would praise the way in which she had carried out her role and say that any change should occur at the end of her reign. In the last months of his prime ministership, though, the ALP embraced an Australian republic as policy at its national conference, and the Australian Republican Movement came into being two weeks later. Hawke said at the time that a republic was inevitable, but he seemed in no hurry to bring it about.

In sharp contrast, new PM Paul Keating was an unabashed republican and derided the presence of the Union Jack on our flag. In 1993 he appointed Malcolm Turnbull to lead an advisory committee, which produced the model for an Australian republic that largely became the formal change put to the people at the 1999 referendum. It proposed that the Queen be replaced by a head of state appointed by the Prime Minister with support from the opposition leader, and ratified by a two-thirds majority of the federal parliament. In essence, the word 'Queen' would be 'whited out' of the Constitution and replaced with 'President', and everything else would remain the same. It was never quite as simple as that, but the description has some plausibility. Essentially it was a minimalist change; most republicans believed that the public would be more likely to vote for a change that was conservative.

Paul Keating's campaign for a republic coincided with a series of embarrassments involving the royal family that combined to damage its public image. Not least of these was the breakdown of Prince Charles's marriage to Princess Diana.

Although most Coalition senators and MPs were monarchists, they were largely lukewarm, and somewhat intimidated by the apparent groundswell of support for republicanism reflected in the opinion polls. A few Liberals came out for a republic. The media was overwhelmingly republican in sentiment. News Limited, Fairfax and the ABC all competed in their advocacy of a change to our form of government. Notable exceptions were radio broadcasters Alan Jones and, to some degree, Neil Mitchell.

Under John Hewson's leadership, the Coalition did not take a clear position. Hewson called the campaign by Keating a diversion from real issues such as economic management – which it was. Nonetheless, it was an important question. When Alexander Downer became leader in 1994, he proposed that if elected the Coalition would hold a constitutional convention, and if a consensus emerged for a particular model, that model would be put to a referendum.

This was an astute move. Like me, Downer was a monarchist, but he sensed that there was significant support for change in the community, and that the issue had to be confronted. I embraced the Downer approach when I became leader again the following year, and it resulted in the referendum of October 1999. This approach allowed time for people to think about the strengths and weaknesses of the current system and the change proposed.

The published opinion polls showed consistent support for a republic until some six weeks before the referendum, when they began to tighten. In the end, the republic was rejected by a margin of 54.13 per cent to 45.13 per cent. Every state voted No, with Victoria recording the narrowest result. The Australian Capital Territory voted for a republic. At the beginning of the campaign, I had feared that the Yes push could well prevail. But the outcome was in line with what I had expected towards the end.

I have often reflected on the referendum since. I was pleased with the result, and in these pages offer some views as to why it turned out as it did. The fierce partisanship of the media probably hurt the republican cause by encouraging Australians' deep scepticism to assert itself: 'If *they're* all in favour, there must be something wrong with it.'

Another major reason for the No vote was the natural conservatism of the Australian people when it comes to constitutional change (discussed earlier in the essay of that name). It's a trite aphorism, but 'If it ain't broke, don't fix it' epitomised the sentiments of many. For a nation that prides itself on social cohesion and political stability, and knows full well that it is one of but a handful of countries to have been continuously democratic for the past 100 years, the idea that Australia needed to be a republic to be truly independent stretched credulity. To invoke a much-loved national expression, it did not pass the pub test.

In a sense it was a case study in why there should always be free votes on certain issues. There was no strong party-political pattern to the result. In Sydney, for example, all the inner-city electorates, both Liberal and Labor, voted solidly Yes. In Wentworth it was 60 per cent, in North Sydney 61 per cent, Bradfield 55 per cent, Grayndler 65 per cent, and in Sydney 68 per cent. Yet in Mitchell, a solid Liberal seat, the No vote was 53 per cent and likewise in Cook. In Gough Whitlam's old seat of Werriwa, the Queen triumphed with 58 per cent of the vote. In contrast, my own electorate of Bennelong endorsed a republic.

There was a like pattern in Melbourne. The inner-city (then) Liberal seats of Kooyong, Higgins and Goldstein all voted strongly republican, with respective support levels of 64 per cent, 63 per cent and 58 per cent. Melbourne, then Labor but now Green, recorded a 70 per cent vote for a republic.

The high personal regard for the Queen, in spite of the issues that had recently beset other members of her family, also played a major role in the republic's defeat. That was in 1999. The esteem in which she is presently held is even greater. If a vote on the issue were to materialise now it would be defeated by a much larger margin. Although unspoken, there is widespread acceptance even among the most zealous republicans that while Elizabeth II remains on the throne there is no likelihood that a change will occur. Those who continue to advocate change always talk about what might happen *after* her reign has ended.

Clearly the passing away of the Queen and, presumably, the accession of the Prince of Wales will be a momentous change. It will end the longest reign in the British monarchy's history. They will never say it, but ardent republicans believe that it will cause an almost immediate fall in support for the institution, simply because Charles will have replaced a much-loved sovereign. They may be right. Then again, they may not. The monarchy is more dynamic than its critics realise.

The new monarch will be a 75- or 80-year-old man. He will from the outset be viewed in a very different light. There will be many who will wish to give him a go. When he ascends the throne, the already immensely popular William and Kate, Duke and Duchess of Cambridge, will be thrust even more into the spotlight.

Now, all of this is speculation, against the hope that the Queen will be with us for some years yet. But the popularity of the current monarch is only one of the two major hurdles that republicans in Australia currently face. The other great hurdle is systemic – that is, the deep division between those who advocate a minimalist approach such as that proposed in the 1999 referendum and those who support the installation of a directly elected president.

I suspect that many of those who voted Yes in 1999 would not have voted that way for a directly elected head of state. Equally, some voted No in 1999 simply because a directly elected head of state was what they wanted.

Embracing a directly elected presidency would radically alter our political system, and for the worse. It would establish a rival power centre. It would raise the prospect of a battle between, say, a Labor PM and a Liberal president, with each claiming the authority of a separate mandate. Given the adversarial character of Australian politics, no detailed restrictions placed on the powers of the president would constrain him or her. A Labor president fresh from a fiercely contested election might not have the power to stop a Liberal PM from doing something he or she opposed, but what would stop him or her from campaigning against it?

Those who support a directly elected presidency could argue that no person who is politically aligned would be allowed to run for the office. How, in a democracy like Australia's, could that be enforced? In any event, it would be profoundly undemocratic to attempt to do so. The presidency would be a public office that any Australian, with whatever support he or she might muster, could aspire to fill. The major political parties would have every right to campaign for a particular candidate.

As I have just written, any directly elected president, with or without the endorsement of a political party, would constitute a separate power source within our national political system. He or she would occupy a prestigious office, have appropriate staff support and facilities, be a guest at numerous public events, enjoy travel entitlements, and inevitably be drawn into political commentary.

It is precisely because the office of Governor-General has been defined by centuries of tradition and precedent, and, crucially, is based on the impartiality of the Crown, that it works so well. The power of the Governor-General does not rival that of the Prime Minister.

Such a heritage would not surround an elected president. Republicans might argue that this is not an issue, as a future president would simply copy the past behaviour of governors-general. The flaw in that argument is that the behaviour of a governor-general is defined by the unique protocols attached to his or her office.

Another argument used by republicans is that becoming a republic would allow us to more sharply identify ourselves in Asia. Over my almost 12 years as PM, I never experienced an identity crisis in my countless dealings with Asian leaders. In 1994, Lee Kuan Yew addressed the republican issue when speaking to the National Press Club. He said: 'I don't think Asia understands what the argument is about. Australia would not generate greater esteem in Asia as a republic than it does with its present constitutional arrangements.' That declaration, from the most formidable political figure produced by South-East Asia since World War II, commands respect.

The republicans' dilemma was illustrated in January 2022, when the Australian Republican Movement released its new Australian Choice Model. It is an attempt to reach a compromise between the direct electionists and the minimalists. It proposes that a president be chosen by a two-thirds majority of a joint sitting of the Senate and House of Representatives. That joint sitting would have before it 11 candidates; the parliament of each state and territory would nominate one, and federal parliament would nominate three. The Australian people would then elect one of the 11 candidates as president. As in the Turnbull model, the president's powers would be similar to those of the Governor-General.

The largely derisive responses to the new plan demonstrated that there can be no compromise, because the approaches are fundamentally different. Even such strong republicans as Paul Keating attacked the model.

Either we upend our current stable system by embracing a directly elected presidency, or we retain the present approach, with the choice of the ceremonial head of government effectively remaining with the Prime Minister of the day (although formally appointed by the Queen).

The current system works. It has served us well.

The essence of our current constitutional monarchy is that the executive – the government – is drawn from and responsible to the legislature, or parliament. It remains in office for as long as it retains a majority in the lower house of the parliament – federally, the House of Representatives. Laws are formally approved by the Governor-General in the name of the Queen. He or she remains apart from the political fray, and discharges important, albeit largely ceremonial functions.

Not only are the ceremonial and executive functions of government separated, but the person discharging the ceremonial functions is also so politically neutral – both in reality and perception – that he or she can act as the ultimate defender of the constitutional integrity of the nation.

Some strong supporters of the monarchy argue that the Governor-General is our head of state. When I was in government, a few of them urged that legislation to this effect be put to the parliament. I resisted this, because it is a constitutionally flawed argument. Laws are enacted in the name of the Queen. Criminal prosecutions are launched and conducted by Crown prosecutors; justice is dispensed in the Queen's courts; MPs take an oath of allegiance to the Queen. It is true that the Governor-General is the effective head of state, given he or she discharges the functions of the monarch simply because the Queen cannot physically do so, any more than she can in Canada or New Zealand. It is instructive that on her various visits to Australia, the Queen has opened parliament, conducted investitures and performed other roles normally undertaken by the Governor-General. When she has done so, the Governor-General has had no role, thus emphasising the representative nature of that office. Under our current constitutional arrangements, however, the only direct function the Queen performs is that of appointing the Governor-General.

It was my custom as PM to have an audience with the Queen whenever she was in Australia, or I was visiting Britain. I imagine that other Australian PMs have done the same. These practices mirror those of the British PM of the day.

The Governor-General is the Queen's representative, but he does not take instructions from her. He exercises the reserve powers of the Crown, completely free of interference. His powers flow from the Australian Constitution. He also acts in accordance with the conventions of the Crown that have been developed and distilled over hundreds of years of constitutional practice. That is one of the reasons why our system of government is so stable. It has evolved over a long period of time. Its history is a strength, not a weakness.

The respective roles of the Queen and the Governor-General were clearly explained by the Queen's private secretary, Sir Martin Charteris, in November 1975, in response to the vote of no confidence in the caretaker Fraser Government. The text of this vote had been conveyed to the Queen, with a request that she intervene. Sir Martin's reply was as follows:

> The Australian Constitution firmly places the
> prerogative powers of the Crown in the hands of the
> Governor-General ... and the Queen has no part in
> the decisions which the Governor-General must take
> in accordance with the Constitution ... it would not
> be proper for her to intervene in person in matters
> which are so clearly placed within the jurisdiction of
> the Governor-General by the Constitution Act.[1]

The push for formal entrenchment of the role of the Governor-General is an unduly defensive response to the claim that our head of state should be 'one of us' – particularly because it is now unthinkable that a future Governor-General should ever be anything else. Since 1965, every Governor-General of Australia has been an Australian. That is not going to change.

What these advocates overlook is that under our system of government, the person who is seen as representing us to the world is the PM. If they would prefer it to be the Governor-General, then they are really arguing for a fundamental change to our system, potentially involving the drawbacks I canvassed earlier.

Retention of the monarchy in Australia remains, as it always has been, a free democratic choice. Periodically, people ask me whether or not we will have the monarchy in 10 years' time. I suggest that they ask me then.

There is no appetite for dumping the monarchy in Australia at present. That will not change for as long as the Queen lives. The end of her reign, at the least, will produce a reflection on our links to arguably the second oldest institution in Western civilisation (after the Holy See). How lasting or how significant that reflection will be, we simply cannot foretell.

THE GREAT AUSTRALIAN DREAM

Reflections on the balanced approach needed to ease Australia's housing problem

My generation, and the two either side, grew up in the belief that if there was a common material aspiration in life, it was to own your own home. For most it became the great Australian dream. It was in my case.

Home ownership as soon as possible after marriage – almost always with a big mortgage – was seen as reinforcing family stability. It was fundamental to 'settling down' and building for the future. The desired home was usually a free-standing dwelling, with a yard and, over time, a Hills Hoist.

It was remarkable that so many Australians on quite modest incomes were able to realise this nirvana. An owner-occupied dwelling became the principal asset most Australians had. To have 'paid off the house' was a common middle-age goal. A sense of relief and security accompanied that final payment to the bank or other lending institution.

However, the special status accorded to home ownership meant that any policies that threatened it met with widespread resistance, even if they were driven by a desire to keep the dream alive for future generations.

Attitudes to home ownership certainly aren't the same the whole world over, though international comparisons must be treated carefully.

Germany is such a case. The home ownership level there sits at a bare 50.4 per cent: surprisingly low for a nation long respected for its economic dynamism. But there are reasons for this, specific to that country. Fully 20 per cent of Germany's private housing stock was destroyed in World War II. Inevitably the rebuilding process involved a bias towards rental housing. That was super-imposed on an entrenched culture of rented apartment living, common to many parts of continental Europe.

At the other end of the spectrum, Romania boasts a private home ownership level of 95.6 per cent, which must seem astonishing to those who associate that country with the utter failure of the Soviet command-economy model. In the communist era, Romania was the antithesis of a property-owning democracy. Yet that is a major reason for the current high level of home ownership. When the old communist regime collapsed, fully 70 per cent of residential properties were owned by the state. To establish a semblance of order amid the resulting chaos, the government offered to sell residences to occupants at very affordable prices, accompanied by many special incentives. The recently liberated children of Lenin were, in a sense, force-fed a diet of Adam Smith.

Switzerland presents as an intriguing case study. Widely regarded not only as affluent and technologically sophisticated, it is also a nation that has successfully remained aloof from Europe's catastrophic wars of the last century. It is constantly seen as a centre of financial stability and discretion. Having 'money in a Swiss bank account' was, for some, a way of hiding true wealth. The Swiss bankers would not tell anyone about this. Perhaps counterintuitively, Switzerland has a very low home-ownership level.

Between 2010 and 2020, it averaged only 43 per cent home ownership, way below most other European nations. The proportion of the population that are renters in Switzerland is the highest in the European Union. It is a small country, but Switzerland's population density is below many other countries with much higher home-ownership levels.

Some attribute this all to wealth inequality; others to the nation's tax system, which treats property owners less generously than renters. Whatever the explanation, the reality is that buying your own home has nothing like the emotional attraction in Switzerland that it has in Australia. The Swiss are very much a nation of apartment dwellers. That is their disposition. I doubt that it will change.

Australia's current level of home ownership sits at 66.4 per cent. As the two comparisons I have invoked suggest, bald levels of home ownership don't tell the full story. However, comparisons with countries that have enjoyed similar levels of political stability and approaches to economic management can provide a more reliable picture. In the UK, the home ownership level is 65.2 per cent, in the US 65.4 per cent and in Canada 68.55 per cent. It is part of the gravitational pull of a middle-class existence in such nations that citizens should want to buy the home in which they (and usually their spouse and children) choose to live.

We are frequently told that the great Australian dream is in danger of disappearing, that home ownership is progressively slipping beyond the reach of even middle- income couples, let alone those less well off. Given the wide acceptance that private home ownership is intrinsic to social stability in Australia, this essay attempts to analyse an issue that remains of concern to so many young people in our society.

Based on a definition of the home ownership rate as being the percentage of residential dwellings that are owner-occupied, either owned outright or with a mortgage, the rate in 1947 in Australia was 53.4 per cent, having been at or slightly below that figure before World War II. It rose sharply to a peak of 71.4 per cent in 1966, from which it has subsided to the current level.

The increase between 1947 and 1966 was dramatic, and due to the rapid middle-classing of Australia during that period. The evidence is that the crude level of ownership has now settled at or below two-thirds. The Household, Income and Labour Dynamics in Australia (HILDA) Survey of 2019 placed Australia 27th among the 38 members of the OECD when it came to home ownership. That was 5 per cent below the OECD average.

The website *Demographia*, administered by two Canadian think tanks, enjoys much respect as an assessor of international housing affordability. It regularly surveys affordability in 92 cities, each with a population over 1 million, across eight countries, namely Australia, the United States, Britain, New Zealand, Ireland, Canada, China and Singapore. The survey measures housing affordability in each city by applying what is called a median multiple. This is a price-to-income ratio, which is the median house price in a city divided by the median household income (pre-tax).

According to the survey of the last quarter of 2021, the least affordable market was Hong Kong, with a median multiple of 23.2. There are some special circumstances that make Hong Kong such an outlier. The authoritarian laws imposed on Hong Kong by Beijing and some related measures have pushed up real estate prices there. The second least affordable was Sydney, at 15.3. This meant that a household in Sydney on the median income needed to earn income at that level for 15.3 years to afford a residence at the median price in the market.

The clear data from these surveys is that housing has become increasingly less affordable in these eight countries in recent years. Although Sydney is the least affordable of the Australian housing markets, Melbourne, with a median multiple of 12.1, was the 88th least affordable of the 92 markets surveyed. Perth was found to have the most affordable market in Australia, yet it was the 73rd least affordable out of the 92.

Whichever way one analyses these survey results, they paint a discouraging picture of housing affordability in Australia. It is of little comfort to observe that housing affordability has also declined in similar societies, especially when the decline in Australia seems to have been more marked.

In June 2021, the median sale price for a house in Australia was $665,000. Average earnings were $90,329 per year, yielding a house-price-to-income ratio of 7.3. Over the past 35 years, the median house price has risen ahead of average earnings, such that the ratio has increased from 3.4 to its mid-2021 level of 7.3.

It has become increasingly hard to buy that first home, especially if incomes are low and there is no credit at the bank of Mum and Dad. Recent data suggest that home ownership rates among 25- to 34-year-olds are only 37 per cent, compared with around 84 per cent for those over 65. The 2016 census revealed that the rate for this group was lower than at any census since 1947. The principal culprit has been the steep increase in the cost of residential units, be they home units, town houses, duplexes or whatever else.

The situation is no easier for those who rent. Although this chapter concentrates on home ownership, there is an equally difficult set of challenges that face those who rent. The two are related and the continuing unaffordability of home ownership inevitably forces more into the rental market. There has been a tendency to overlook the difficulties faced by a growing cohort of renters who, because of the ever-rising cost of housing, have stayed much longer paying rent than they might have expected. Renting in transition has become, for them, renting indefinitely. Between 1997–1998 and 2017–2018, the proportion of private renters in Australia rose from 20 to 27 per cent of the population. That remarkable movement not only reflected the increase in housing costs, but throws light on the state of the private rental market.

Although this is not a chapter on the state of that market, it should be noted that this is a domain where positive interaction between federal and state policies has been lacking. Laws governing the landlord–tenant relationship have always been the responsibility of the states. Both levels of government play a part in providing social housing, with state governments usually wanting the Commonwealth to write a cheque and then vacate the scene. Federal governments more recently have discharged their role through rent assistance payments to tenants. As in many areas, greater cooperation and policy coordination is needed.

There are several reasons for the surge in the cost of housing over the past 20 years. For much of that period, interest rates have been at historic lows. This has boosted borrowing capacity, which in turn has increased buying power. But supply has not matched that increased demand, with obvious consequences for the cost of housing. Low interest rates are also seen as encouraging speculative investment in housing, thus inflating house prices to the detriment of the 'genuine' home buyer.

It is important, though, that the impact of low interest rates be kept in perspective. Increases in house prices can largely offset the benefits of low interest rates over time. For example, a house costing $172,000 in June 2001 – the then median price – with a mortgage at 80 per cent of its value, carrying an interest rate of 13.2 per cent, meant that 42.1 per cent of average weekly earnings was consumed in servicing the loan. In June 2021, an equivalent loan with an interest rate of 4.5 per cent still consumed 38.8 per cent of average weekly earnings. By then the median house price had risen to $665,000. Mortgage costs as a percentage of earnings peaked in 2008 at over 50 per cent and have hovered between 37 per cent and 39 per cent since 2013. Yet average property prices have more than doubled, as a multiple of average household disposable income, over the past 30 years, after that ratio had been reasonably stable over the previous 30 to 40 years.

Another explanation advanced by many for the surge in housing prices is the high rate of immigration, which has fallen recently only because of the pandemic. Net overseas migration averaged 80,000 a year from 1901 to 2018, yet for most of the past two decades it was way above this figure, peaking at 320,000 in 2011. If current policy attitudes, which appear to be bipartisan, obtain, then migration will soon resume its upward trajectory.

Levels of migration have implications for a wide range of policy areas beyond housing affordability, and there are significant benefits in ensuring that they remain high. One of the many arguments for high immigration is that it can help to slow the progressive ageing of the population, as the bulk of newcomers are of a younger demographic.

When my government was in power it pursued policies such as the much-derided 'baby bonus' to ease the additional costs associated with having children. These were progressively removed, or scaled back, by later governments, and in the process wrongly described as 'middle-class welfare'. They were nothing of the kind. Not only did they help with the costs of having children, but they also provided greater choice for parents on medium and low incomes over the caring arrangements for their young children.

Australia's fertility rate rose while those policies were in effect. It peaked at 1.81 in 2006. It now stands at 1.58.[1] If those now largely abandoned policies produced such an outcome, then the obvious conclusions are that not only should such an approach never have been discarded, but also, if it is a national goal to slow the ageing of the population, then lifting the fertility rate is superior to migration. Suffice it to say that they should never be seen as mutually exclusive.

Even if high immigration is in some ways beneficial, it is hard to dispute the fact that the elevated migration levels of the past 20 years have put upward pressure on the cost of housing. New migrants often arrive as family groups and their need for housing is frequently immediate. This can put pressure on housing in large urban centres in particular, because of their attractions for new migrants in search of employment. Other countries with similar political and economic histories have enjoyed equally low interest rates over recent years, yet have not experienced such a sharp increase in housing costs. That could be because those nations have not had such high levels of immigration as Australia.

Many argue that taxation policies with a generic application, such as negative gearing and the capital gains tax discount of 50 per cent for individuals who own an asset for 12 months or more, have also hiked up housing costs, because they encourage speculative investment in housing.

Yet the sober reality is that many of the essential causes of expensive housing in Australia are already 'baked into' the system. In a sense the great Australian dream has collided with the great Australian paradox. We are one of the most urbanised nations in the world. Ours is a huge country with a small population, the bulk of which is crammed into a few large cities. Australians like living in the suburbs of the big cities. Over the years, state governments have relocated public service jobs and offered incentives to encourage more people to live in the regions. Cheaper housing will also draw some to regional areas. Indeed, the combination of less expensive housing and the increased incidence of working from home spawned by the pandemic has produced some signs of a drift away from the cities. None of these things, though, will shift the fundamentals.

The planning policies of state governments have only aggravated the problem. There is always political pressure on a state government to avoid policy decisions that might reduce the value of existing housing stock in an area. As a result, green-belt areas have proliferated, and new land releases have lagged behind demand. The interests of current home owners are always preferred to those of new entrants. After all, there are a lot more of them. Like observations can be made of the decisions of local councils. These realities have been with us for generations and have been getting worse as the populations of our large cities continue to increase.

All of this leads to the fundamental question of what can be done to reduce the cost of housing or, perhaps more realistically, prevent housing from becoming even less affordable in the future.

When housing affordability is debated, it is all about the level of interest rates and stamp duty, and whether there should be a grant for first home buyers, or minimum allowable deposits. That nothing can be done to stop the rise of house prices is a given.

It was at the 1963 election that the Menzies Government initially put forward a first home buyer's grant of £250. Since then, such grants have come and gone, with support from both sides of politics. The tax deductibility of interest payments has also enjoyed several outings. Interest rates are so low now that this policy is not raised any more, but that might change if rates begin to climb. Legislative changes to remove or modify negative gearing and the 50 per cent capital gains tax discount continue to be raised as possible solutions.

Most students of this broad policy area have reached the conclusion that while such initiatives have helped individuals, usually in a modest fashion, they have not acted to reduce the overall cost of housing. In many cases they have in fact put upward pressure on housing prices through increasing demand. These issues will continue to be debated, but there is little doubt that none of them, individually or in combination, represents the silver bullet so earnestly sought for housing affordability.

Nevertheless, some specific measures could be adopted to help moderate the unacceptably high cost of housing for first-time buyers. I canvass them here against the overarching imperative of pursuing sound fiscal, monetary and taxation policies, allied to other approaches that encourage growth and investment.

I am attracted to the taxation proposal of the New South Wales Premier Dominic Perrottet to progressively replace stamp duty on residential real estate with land tax. The present stamp duty is a heavy initial impost, which disproportionately burdens those buying their first home.

The ill-judged policies of state and local governments over many decades have left their legacy of needlessly high housing prices. It is unrealistic to imagine that their accumulated impact can be rolled back, but state governments and local councils should place a high priority on reversing those policies for the future. The goal should be to *expand* the urban sprawl, not restrict it. This will meet with stiff resistance, but it is essential to any serious reform. This goal should be allied to steps to relax land-use protocols and formulate a generally accelerated approval process at state and local government levels.

On the regulatory front, there is a case for tighter controls on lending by banks and other lenders to those who are borrowing more than they can service if they encounter income headwinds. All this does though is to protect borrowers against the consequences of their own legitimate desire to share the dream.

I remain a strong supporter of high immigration, but, consistent with a return to increased levels, it should be possible to factor in the capacity of the Australian economy to absorb new settlers.

At the recent election, Labor proposed a policy under which eligible home buyers would receive an equity contribution of up to 40 per cent of the purchase price of a new home and up to 30 per cent for an existing home. The home buyer would need to have a deposit of 2 per cent and qualify for a standard home loan to finance the remainder of the purchase. The scheme would be available to individuals with a taxable income of up to $90,000 for individuals and $120,000 for couples. A condition of the policy was that the government would recover its equity and its share of the capital gain when the house is sold. Only 10,000 Australians per year would be eligible.

By contrast, the Coalition proposed that first home buyers could invest up to 40 per cent of their superannuation, to a maximum of $50,000. To be eligible a buyer must have saved a minimum 5 per cent of the deposit. There was no income limit, and couples could use their combined savings. In addition, the Coalition proposed to lower the age threshold for those who could access downsizing contributions to superannuation from 60 to 55.

Neither policy, if fully implemented, would significantly increase the affordability of housing in Australia, although both approaches carry the potential to modestly assist some in buying their first home. I assume that the Albanese Government will implement Labor's policy. Given the reverence it has for the current superannuation arrangements, and especially the stake of the large union-dominated industry funds, it is unlikely to allow potential home buyers access to any portion of their superannuation.

There is no silver bullet. The present housing market in Australia is a classic case study of what happens to price when demand runs ahead of supply. Governments can help with grants and tax breaks, but they will have little impact beyond the margin. Ensuring that the economy functions efficiently and with low inflation and optimum employment opportunities will do more than anything to keep home ownership within the reach of modest and middle-income earners.

9/11: TWENTY-ONE YEARS ON

Reflections on balancing stability and autonomy in Afghanistan and Iraq

There have been three unexpected, dramatic and/or tragic events in my lifetime that have prompted the question 'Where were you when?' Those events were the assassination of President John Kennedy in 1963, the 1975 dismissal of Gough Whitlam by Sir John Kerr, and the 2001 terrorist attacks on New York and Washington DC.

All three came without warning. All had lasting consequences of a mixed political and social kind, both domestically and internationally.

On the morning of Saturday 23 November 1963, I was at home in Earlwood, Sydney, where I lived with my mother. I was preparing to do some campaigning for the 30 November federal election with Tom Hughes QC, the

Liberal candidate for the local electorate of Parkes. The phone rang at about 8.30 am. It was my brother Bob, who simply said: 'Kennedy's been shot dead in Dallas.' It was shocking news, and provided a completely surreal atmosphere to campaigning from the back of a truck near Campsie Railway Station later that morning.

I had been an MP for just 18 months when Whitlam was sacked. I had followed every twist and turn of the great constitutional saga that came to a climax that day, 11 November 1975. I was in the House of Representatives chamber, waiting for the afternoon sitting to commence, when I encountered Vic Garland, the Chief Opposition Whip. He said to me: 'Kerr's sacked Gough.' I found it hard to believe. Several minutes later, the bells to announce the sitting stopped ringing, and when the Speaker called Malcolm Fraser – describing him as 'the Honourable Member for Wannon', not 'the Leader of the Opposition' – I knew that Garland had been right. Fraser had been commissioned by the Governor-General as caretaker PM. Fraser then addressed the house, explaining what had happened. I was shocked. Most of my colleagues were as well, although some would later reconstruct events to demonstrate that they had known all along that this would be the outcome.

As is well known, I was in Washington, as PM, on 11 September 2001. I had travelled to the US capital to address a joint sitting of Congress on 12 September, marking the 50th anniversary of the ANZUS Treaty between our two nations and New Zealand. That morning I went for my usual walk, during which I talked on the phone to Peter Costello about the pending collapse of Ansett, then by far the biggest story in Australia. When I returned, I had a brief discussion with my press secretary, Tony O'Leary, about a news conference scheduled for later that morning, largely for the Australian media travelling with us. We expected that Ansett would be the main topic that the media would want to raise.

At the end of the discussion, O'Leary told me a plane had just hit one of the towers of the World Trade Center in New York. We quickly agreed that it was a terrible accident.

Some 20 minutes later, he was banging on my door.

When I opened it, he said: 'You'd better turn on the TV. Another plane has hit the second tower.' Now we both knew that this was no accident.

Turning on the TV, we looked in horror at the burning World Trade Center. I went ahead with the news conference, and at the beginning I made a brief reference to what had just happened in New York.

It was during the conference that the third hijacked plane slammed into the Pentagon. When the conference finished, the blinds were pulled back and smoke could be seen rising from that direction.

My first thought was for Janette and our son Tim, who had come over from London, where he was temporarily working. They had gone out sight-seeing early, and I knew that they had wanted to see the Robert E. Lee Memorial, which is not far from the Pentagon.

My security detail later told me that they were okay and had been taken to a safe house. They subsequently joined me in the bunker under the Australian Embassy.

I have provided this detail of the hours leading up to these epoch-changing attacks to underline the fact that they were completely unexpected. This was a series of audaciously planned and executed terrorist acts that rocked America to its core, and whose effects reverberated around the world. It created new fears. It permanently changed aspects of our lives. It reassembled old alliances and elevated intelligence-gathering to a higher order, so that, in the past 20 years, timely intelligence has become our most effective weapon in fighting terrorism.

Without doubt, being in Washington when it all happened intensified my emotional reaction. The joint sitting of Congress that I had been scheduled to address the next day became instead the forum for a united expression of condemnation of the attacks and support for considered measures against those responsible. The impact of attending that sitting was immense. I was deeply moved by the standing ovation I received. Fortuitously, through my presence, I was able to convey both friendship and support in a bewildering and, yes, isolating hour for our American friends.

When I spoke to the media that day before leaving the US, I said this:

In many respects, yesterday marked the end of an era of a degree of innocence following the end of the Cold War and a decade in which it seemed as though things which posed a continuous threat were behind us. But regrettably we now face a possibility of a period in which the threat of terrorism will be with us in the way the threat of a nuclear war was around for so long before the end of the Cold War. I think it is as bad as that and I don't think any of us should pretend otherwise.

With the benefit of 20 years of hindsight, I would not alter one word of that judgement.

During that news conference I also affirmed that Australia would support America in any appropriate response to the attacks. I said: 'just because you are big and strong doesn't mean that you can't feel lonely, and you can't feel that your heart has been ripped out. And I think that it is very important, therefore, that Americans know that they have got some really good, reliable friends.' It was an occasion not just to be an 80 per cent ally, but a 100 per cent one.[1]

Travelling back to Australia on Air Force Two – the first aeroplane to leave US airspace after the attacks – I discussed the situation at length with Alexander Downer. The Foreign Minister suggested that Australia invoke the ANZUS Treaty, whose 50th anniversary we had ironically just been prevented from celebrating.

I readily agreed. A terrorist attack on the metropolitan territory of one of the signatories clearly came within the provisions of the treaty. The minister and I agreed to recommend this to cabinet when it met the following day in Canberra.

After this discussion I walked back to where Tom Schieffer, the US Ambassador to Australia, was sitting on the plane and told him of the discussion. He understood its significance and was visibly touched. The treaty had always been seen primarily as the instrument through which *the US* would defend *Australia*, so it was both ironic and symbolic that the first time it would be invoked was by Australia because of an attack on America.

Downer and I both agreed that if the time came, Australia would offer military support to any retaliation by the US. The cabinet readily endorsed the invoking of the ANZUS Treaty, and I announced that decision the same day, 14 September.

There was plenty of intelligence material indicating that the terrorist group Al Qaeda – operating out of Afghanistan with support from that country's fundamentalist rulers, the Taliban – was responsible for the 9/11 attacks. A bare few hours after the three planes had wreaked their havoc, that was the consensus in Washington, and in intelligence circles around the world.

Discussions between American and Australian military figures began early. There was an understanding that once US forces were ready to retaliate, if help were needed, Australia was a highly favoured partner. George Bush made this very clear to me at the APEC Summit in Shanghai in October (which will feature again in the next essay).

The early stages of the operation in Afghanistan were authorised by a UN resolution and involved the use of modest special forces from the US, with help from the British and a contingent of 150 Australians. Local forces from the Northern Alliance, a collection of the Taliban's enemies from within the country, were also part of the initial foray. The Americans had always wanted to involve the international community, as well as the Afghans themselves, in the future of the country. We provided refuelling capacity for our allies, as well as a group of F/A 18 Hornets, based on the British–American Indo-Pacific military base of Diego Garcia.

The Australian commitment reflected a common-sense assessment of our nation's capacity and interests. We had special responsibilities closer to home, notably our leadership of the International Force for East Timor, sent into the country soon after its vote for independence in

1999. The very success of that mission meant that the world increasingly saw Australia as playing a significant role in our part of the world. We could commit modest numbers of highly trained and skilled personnel as part of coalition operations in different areas of the world in pursuit of a common objective. We could be a reliable international partner but take care to avoid overreach. As part of this understanding, we naturally accepted that the more powerful coalition partner called the shots.

There was healthy support in Australia for the initial military operation in Afghanistan. A Newspoll of 31 October reported that 66 per cent of Australians were in favour.[2] It also enjoyed bipartisan parliamentary support. The Labor opposition, led by Kim Beazley, was strongly behind it throughout the 2001 election campaign, held in October and November.

The US and its allies launched their attack on Afghanistan in early October. This early military operation was highly successful, and by December, Taliban control of the country had collapsed. Most of our personnel came home at the end of 2002, and increasingly the Americans saw their role as being one of consolidation and reconstruction.

On 27 November, the United Nations convened a meeting in Bonn, Germany, that did not include the Taliban. This meeting installed Hamad Karzai as head of an interim administration. Major advances for women were later written into a new constitution, and on 20 December overall control of the Western military presence was transferred to the International Security Assistance Force (ISAF), which was largely a NATO operation.

As time passed, the argument developed that the US, having demolished the Taliban and ensured as best it could that Afghanistan would never again provide a launching pad for an Al Qaeda 9/11-type attack, then mistakenly decided to export Western-style democracy to the country. Given that the original objective of the invasion was to destroy the group responsible for the 9/11 attack, I always found it hard to accept that the Americans would, as a deliberate act of policy, set about trying to install a Western democratic system in a country quite unfamiliar with such governance. It made sense that the US and its allies would hold and consolidate the gains from their initial attack, and that in the process some democratic forms would be introduced. A new government had to be installed. This occurred under the aegis of the international community. As already explained, the United Nations played a major role.

The more prosaic explanation is that measures to preserve the gains of late 2001 had to go beyond the strictly military. Improving local governance and services, confronting the most egregious forms of corruption, building economic confidence and offering Afghans the hope of a better life were crucial to preserving the dividend of having seen off the Taliban and Al Qaeda. A local community that had been forced to endure intimidation and threats from the Taliban and still faced the prospect that the Taliban would return needed an incentive to resist them. That incentive could only be provided by a friendly foreign military presence, or a better trained and equipped local Afghan military. In practice, that is what happened. It was a policy of holding on to gains and strengthening the capacity of the locals to withstand future attacks.

It is worth noting some of the views of Donald Rumsfeld, then the US Defense Secretary. In his memoir *Known and Unknown* he wrote:

> *My position is that we were not in Afghanistan to transform a deeply conservative Islamic culture into a model of liberal modernity. We were not there to eradicate corruption or to end poppy cultivation …* *Afghans would need to take charge of their own fate. Afghans would build their own society the way they wanted.*[3]

Rumsfeld summarised the US attitude thus: 'Our more modest goal was to rid Afghanistan of Al Qaeda and replace their Taliban hosts with a government which would not harbour terrorists. We were willing to let Afghan traditions and processes determine the political outcomes.'[4]

When, in 2005, my government announced that a new force of some 150 Australian Defence Force personnel was going into Afghanistan because of the deterioration in that country's security position, I said that their task would be similar to that of the personnel who had been sent late in 2001. At my joint news conference on 13 July 2005 with Robert Hill, the Defence Minister, I remarked, 'It's fair to say that the progress that's been made and the establishment of a legitimate government in Afghanistan has come under increasing attack and pressure from the Taliban in particular and some elements of Al Qaeda.'[5] The aim was still to preserve what had been achieved.

That stance was confirmed after the change of government in Australia in November 2007. Speaking to the Brookings Institute on 16 July 2008, the new ALP Defence Mnister, Joel Fitzgibbon, said:

> *Australia remains committed to the Afghanistan project. We believe it goes to the heart of our own national security at a time when we are all facing a changing strategic environment. We are committed to ensuring that a tyrannical regime which provides safe haven for terrorists cannot take hold in Afghanistan again. Quite apart from how we limit the capabilities of terrorists who wish to do harm to our citizens, we have delivered real benefits in terms of education,*

health care and employment to the people of
Afghanistan. We have protected our own people but
made the lives of ordinary Afghans better which is a
cause worth continuing.[6]

Those words could easily have been uttered by Brendan Nelson, the Defence Minister in the recently defeated Coalition government.

Here, perhaps, we are talking about a distinction without a difference. At what point did predictable and essential measures to shore up gains against the Taliban begin to look like nation-building? The US had no alternative but to embrace them. It was inconceivable for the Americans to have announced that they were going home, without being able to credibly claim that they were leaving behind an Afghan government ready and able to prevent the re-emergence of the Taliban. Apart from anything else, such a move would have been heavily criticised in their own country. They had no alternative but to stay and do as they did.

Al Qaeda leader Osama Bin Laden had avoided capture in 2001 and found safety in Pakistan. He would ultimately be tracked to the city of Abbottabad and killed in 2011. Throughout the 20-year US involvement in Afghanistan, an uneasy ambiguity existed in relation to Pakistan. There was much evidence of support and succour flowing from Islamabad to the Taliban. Pakistan's close relationship with

China also bothered the Americans, who were reluctant to push the Pakistanis too far, lest that relationship deepen. To complicate matters, Pakistan was a nuclear-armed state. As I write, that uneasy ambiguity persists.

Meanwhile, in early 2002, the US had begun to contemplate an attack on Iraq, for reasons I will turn to soon. Critics argue that it was around this point that the US, Australia and others were diverted from Afghanistan, because of their growing preoccupation with Iraq, and that if this had not happened then suppression of the Taliban would have been completed and the US and others would have withdrawn many years earlier, leaving a viable and stable country behind.

A flaw in that argument is that the original objectives in Afghanistan had been achieved well before the invasion of Iraq in March 2003. Those objectives had been to root out Al Qaeda and cripple the Taliban. In fact, as Donald Rumsfeld wrote in *Known and Unknown*, 'it was precisely during the toughest period in the Iraq war that Afghanistan, with coalition help, took some of its most promising steps toward a free and better future'.[7]

Another, even greater flaw in those critics' argument is that despite the initial success, groups such as the Taliban and Al Qaeda were never likely to be completely contained in a nation as tribal and fractured as Afghanistan, particularly given the dubious role of neighbouring Pakistan. Without an improved local military capacity, coupled with a political system that enjoyed the confidence of the Afghan people, there was always the prospect that the movement would regroup and return. Given the character and history of that nation, achieving what was necessary to suppress the Taliban in a lasting way was truly daunting.

Over time, those same critics would conveniently label Afghanistan the 'good' war and Iraq the 'bad' one.

Iraqi dictator Saddam Hussein was not complicit in the 9/11 attacks. In all the discussions I had with President Bush, he never claimed that. Nor can I recall any other senior member of the Bush Administration who did so.

It is frequently forgotten that the desire to remove Saddam was a bipartisan objective of US foreign policy before 9/11. In 1998 Congress enacted the *Iraq Liberation Act*, which was signed into law by President Bill Clinton. Under its provisions, the President was required to nominate specific groups in Iraq that could receive assistance from the US.

This enactment had massive Democrat and Republican support, passing the House of Representatives by 360 to 38, and the Senate without opposition. It recited Saddam's past transgressions, particularly his human-rights abuses, and envisaged a democratic Iraq once Saddam had gone. Passage of this Act was driven by gathering anger at Saddam's repeated non-cooperation with UN weapons inspectors, and lingering regrets that after the Americans had expelled the Iraqis from Kuwait in 1991 they had not gone on to Baghdad and removed the Iraqi dictator.

Saddam was well and truly unfinished business when the 9/11 attacks occurred. He might not have been involved in those heinous acts, but they signalled to many Americans that he might do something just as bad or even worse in the future.

Addressing the General Assembly on 12 September 2002, President Bush said that 'our greatest fear is that terrorists will find a short cut to their mad ambitions when an outlaw regime supplies them with the technologies to kill on a massive scale'.[8] That sentence encapsulated American fears about Iraq. Having experienced the 9/11 attacks, who could blame the citizens of the US from thinking that the next time a hijacked plane headed for a tall building it might be carrying a chemical, biological or even nuclear weapon sourced from Iraq?

Most senior US figures believed that Saddam had weapons of mass destruction (WMDs). That is what the intelligence had indicated. My government's decision to join the US-led invasion of Iraq was the most difficult it ever took. It was intensely unpopular, and left me and my colleagues politically exposed when stockpiles of WMDs were *not* found.

Yet I have never wavered in my belief that that decision was right. There was a justifiable fear that Saddam would pass on some of the WMDs he was believed to possess to a terrorist group, which would then use them against the United States or others. The events of 9/11 dramatically intensified this fear. Likewise, I have always said that the closeness of our relationship with the Americans featured prominently in our decision to send forces to Iraq.

Without question the failure to find stockpiles of WMDs in Iraq was held against the Bush Administration and its coalition partners, such as Australia. It was alleged that, in our determination to remove Saddam, we mounted an illegal invasion that fractured the international community. The legal advice given to the government was that the military operation mounted in Iraq fell within the authorisation contained in resolutions 687 and 1441, the first of which was passed at the time of the first Gulf War.

Certainly, the intelligence failure was a major one. Although extensive WMD programs were found, establishing that Iraq had the *capacity* to readily manufacture and assemble WMDs, no physical WMDs could be located. This was a painful embarrassment for the Americans, strengthened the hands of the many European critics of President Bush, poisoned all subsequent media coverage of events in Iraq and immeasurably emboldened the recruiting efforts of the anti-American forces inside Iraq.

At the extreme end, critics of the invasion claimed that the US and its allies had distorted, misrepresented or even invented intelligence, and that therefore the invasion had been based on a lie. That claim was without any foundation, though the failure to find stockpiles gave it additional credence in the eyes of many.

In general, Australia's intelligence agencies had believed that WMDs existed, although the Defence Intelligence Organisation had held less strongly to the view. Several independent inquiries found no evidence that Australian agencies had manufactured intelligence, had presented it in a particular light or had been subjected to political interference or pressure.

The prime intelligence sources had been American and to some degree British. In October 2002, a then-secret National Intelligence Assessment (NIA) had consolidated the views of all the US intelligence agencies, including the CIA. Its key judgements included the following:

> *We judge that Iraq has continued its weapons of*
> *mass destruction (WMD) programs in defiance*
> *of UN resolutions and restrictions. Baghdad has*
> *chemical and biological weapons as well as missiles*
> *with ranges in excess of UN restrictions; if left*
> *unchecked, it probably will have a nuclear weapon*
> *during this decade. (See alternative INR view at the*
> *end of these key judgements.)*
>
> *We judge that we are seeing only a portion of Iraq's*
> *WMD efforts, owing to Baghdad's vigorous denial and*

deception efforts. Since inspections ended in 1998, Iraq
has maintained its chemical weapons effort, energizes
[sic] its missile program, and invested more heavily
in biological weapons; in the view of most agencies,
Baghdad is reconstituting its nuclear weapons program.[9]

The NIA asserted that Saddam, if sufficiently desperate, might decide that only an organisation such as Al Qaeda – which had worldwide reach and extensive terrorist infrastructure, and was already engaged in a life-or-death struggle against the United States – could perpetrate the type of terrorist attack that he would hope to conduct.

The alternative INR view mentioned above was from the intelligence unit of the State Department, and related to the unit's view that Iraq had not tried to source uranium yellowcake from Niger. Separate British intelligence established that it had. I relied on the British intelligence when I made the claim in a speech.

An eternal dilemma always surrounds intelligence assessments and how governments respond to them. They never produce evidence beyond a reasonable doubt. Almost always, the art of intelligence assessment involves assembling a mosaic of varying, incomplete and sometimes contradictory sources. To insist on a still higher standard of proof could well prevent an Iraq-style intelligence failure in the future, but it could have other consequences too. In the final analysis, those holding executive power must make the judgement call.

Let me illustrate. In his book *The Finish: The Killing of Osama Bin Laden*, journalist Mark Bowden quotes the Deputy Director of the CIA, Michael Morrell, as telling President Barack Obama that he had spent a lot of time on both WMDs and the tracing of Bin Laden, 'and I am telling you the case for WMDs wasn't just stronger, it was much stronger'.[10]

To his great credit, Obama authorised the operation in Pakistan that disposed of Bin Laden. History would have been very unkind to the President if he had adopted the literal implications of the Deputy Director's advice. It could be said with even greater force that if President Bush had held back and Saddam had possessed WMDs that were handed to a terrorist group then used against the US, he would have been forever damned by history.

Yet it was the internal chaos following Saddam's removal that did the most damage, first and foremost to the wellbeing of the Iraqi people but also to the credibility of those who had taken the decision to invade. The terrorist attacks that occurred in the nation for several years afterwards claimed many thousands of innocent lives and weighed even more heavily on the US and its allies than the original invasion. Those attacks were largely carried out or inspired by Saddam loyalists.

Regrettably, their cause was greatly aided by the decisions in 2003 of the new US head of the Coalition Provisional Authority, Paul Bremer, to purge Baathists, a group totally sympathetic to Saddam Hussein, from the civil service, and then to disband the Iraqi army and intelligence service. These decisions were ill judged and, among other things, put well-armed and very disaffected Sunni Iraqis onto the streets. They were ready recruits for the anti-American insurgency that would persist for several years.

Bremer's edicts robbed the country of much of its administrative infrastructure. Critically, they ignored the lessons of history. I have never forgotten Lee Kuan Yew's personal account to me of how few Japanese were installed in key positions after the fall of Singapore in 1942. A premium was placed on preserving order. In the interests of stability, Tokyo left the locals largely in place.

The reputation of the Americans in Iraq was further stained by revelations in 2004 of abuse of Iraqi prisoners in Abu Ghraib jail by a small number of US personnel.

Despite the continuing chaos, there was a 75 per cent turnout at the first nationwide elections held in Iraq in January 2005. In December of that year, Saddam was captured, brought to trial, found guilty and executed, all according to the Iraqi judicial system.

Despairing of the deteriorating security situation, President Bush embraced a surge in 2007, sending more than 20,000 additional troops to Iraq. The operation was overseen by General David Petraeus, an impressive military leader and counter-insurgency expert, whom I met in Baghdad that year. Despite the scepticism of many senior US military figures, the surge was very successful, and Petraeus was later made supremo of operations in both Iraq and Afghanistan. The surge's success was influenced by the Sunni Awakening two years earlier, in which Sunni leaders in Al Anbar Province had joined forces with the majority-Shia Iraqi Government to fight Al Qaeda and other insurgent groups. It was a signal that future cooperation between Shias and Sunnis was possible.

Barack Obama was elected in 2009 with a policy to withdraw from Iraq as soon as possible. He always distanced himself from Bush's decision to go into Iraq, and his presidential successor, Donald Trump, was also a critic from early in the war. Neither was a member of Congress when in 2002, by a large margin, it voted to authorise military action against Iraq. By the time Obama and Trump were respectively major contenders for the White House, the war had long since soured politically. It was not difficult for either of them to attack Bush over Iraq.

When US troops finally left in 2011, their combat deaths had reached 4000. At least 100,000 Iraqis had been killed in the domestic conflict that followed the US invasion.

Regrettably, the Shia-dominated government in Iraq would show bad faith, fail to pay the Sunnis who had been incorporated into the national military, and generally reassert its sectarian ascendancy. There is a credible view that if the US had maintained a military presence in Iraq for longer, this betrayal by the Shia majority would not have occurred. Obama's critics have also claimed that he forced the pace on withdrawal, which stimulated the rise of the ultra-violent jihadist group ISIS in both Iraq and Syria around 2014. The strong alternative view is that the US invasion had so destabilised Iraq that the conditions were ripe for the emergence of this group, with its extremist dogma and practices. Yet the common threat posed by ISIS, as well as pressure from the Americans, did produce better policy making in Baghdad.

There was evidence that Iraq was slowly stabilising; 2018 saw record levels of oil production. But the country was still beset by random violence. The leadership of Mustafa Al-Kadhimi, the current Prime Minister of Iraq, who is pro-American but conscious of the overbearing proximity of Iran, offers hope – if he can last in that post. He believes in democracy and the critical need for the Shias, Sunnis and Kurds to work together. He won much praise as head of Iraqi intelligence between 2016 and 2020.

To those who are constantly critical of American and Australian policy in Afghanistan I have two things to say. There was overwhelming domestic and world support for the

US military action in late 2001. It was a justified response in every way. Secondly, the prime objective of destroying Al Qaeda in Afghanistan and ensuring a 9/11-type attack could not be launched from there again was achieved. With the passage of time those ever-salient realities tend to be forgotten.

Since then, American prestige has been further dented by the chaotic end of the US presence in Afghanistan. The desire of the American public to be done with a war that seemed as if it would never end was understandable, but the final achievement of that desire was nothing short of shambolic.

How the US left Afghanistan was always going to be at least as important as *when* it left. In 2009, when President Obama announced that he was sending tens of thousands more US troops to the country, he also unwisely nominated a withdrawal date of 18 months later. This was essentially an invitation to the Taliban to wait out the infidel. Donald Trump also made a big mistake in declaring that the US was leaving before he had struck a bargain with the Taliban. That was not the art of a good deal.

Finally, in 2021, President Biden oversaw a clumsy end, by not making the withdrawal conditional upon the extraction of locals whom America and its allies wanted to assist. A satisfactory evacuation of all of those deemed at risk should have governed the withdrawal date, not the reverse. The distressing images of Afghans running beside a taxiing

US Globemaster will endure as a propaganda tool for those who despise the US and all it stands for. Sadly, that will be the lasting image of America's withdrawal from Afghanistan.

Writing in 2020, Robert Gates, Defense Secretary to both Bush and Obama and a former director of the CIA, delivered the following judgement on 18 years of US involvement in Afghanistan:

> *After 18 years of nation-building and tens of billions of dollars in assistance, Afghanistan can hardly be considered a success story. The picture is not all bad, though. In 2001 there were one million students in Afghan schools, all of them male. In 2017, there were 8.4 million students, 40% of them female. In 2008, more than 57% of the population lived within a one hour walk to a health facility, up from 9% in 2002, largely due to USAID efforts. The under-five mortality rate decreased from 87 per 1000 live births in 2005 to 55 per 1000 in 2015.*[11]

Gates went on to point out that, despite the security situation, elections continued to be held. Many women had started businesses and, notwithstanding the high casualties, Afghan men continued to enlist in the army and police force in order to fight the Taliban. Due to the roles he had held, Gates's judgement carried a lot of authority.

With the Taliban now returned to power, pessimism about the future of Afghanistan is understandable. It is hard to believe that the Taliban have turned over a new page. Yet it will not be easy for them to remove the gains of the past 15 to 20 years, particularly those made by women. The new rulers will need the favour of the international community. They will find that there is more to running a country than firing bullets into the air. Foreign investment as well as aid will be crucial. Separately, there is the inherently fragmented character of the country. Tribalism, ethnic rivalries and religious differences remain. We cannot know how readily terrorism will re-germinate. These issues are now the Taliban's to confront.

The depressing reality, though, is that the Taliban is back in charge, albeit in a very different world. There are disheartening signs that the women of Afghanistan are again being denied some fundamental rights. The country's economy continues to weaken. Yet it is hard to imagine that Afghanistan will, in the foreseeable future, facilitate a terrorist attack of anything approaching the scale of 9/11.

Twenty years after 9/11 we are now better prepared against terrorism than once was the case. We fully understand that timely intelligence is the best defensive weapon in fighting it. The world will never fully comprehend just how many potential terrorist attacks that timely intelligence has aborted over those two decades.

THE CHINA DILEMMA

**Reflections on the balance between
supporting our major ally and dealing
with our major trading partner**

The 2001 APEC Economic Leaders' Meeting, held in
Shanghai on 20 and 21 October, was remarkable for several
reasons. It was held only three weeks before an Australian
federal election, scheduled for 10 November 2001. It was the
first ever held in China. And it took place just weeks after
the 9/11 terrorist attacks on New York and Washington that
were the focus of the previous chapter.

Although I had to interrupt my election campaign to be
at the meeting, I had no hesitation in going. Australia had
to be represented by its head of government at the largest
gathering of world leaders since the shocking US terror
attacks that had rocked the politics of the globe.

During the 20 years that have passed since that summit, I have often reflected on the circumstances in which it was held. The preoccupation of Americans and many others was when and where the next attack of that kind might occur. This common apprehension united the nations whose leaders gathered in China's most prosperous, cosmopolitan and international city.

It was in Shanghai 80 years earlier that the Chinese Communist Party had been launched. The irony of the fact that this meeting was taking place under the auspices of a totalitarian regime that had ruthlessly governed the most populous country in the world since 1949 was not lost on those attending. Certainly not on George Walker Bush, 45th President of the United States. As he and I observed the total absence of traffic in the streets surrounding us, he said to me: 'Gee, John, you wouldn't get away with that in New York.'

To which I responded, 'Nor Sydney.'

Our host was the cagey but likeable Jiang Zemin, President of China and Secretary-General of the Chinese Communist Party since 1993. He had risen, unexpectedly, to a position of power after the turmoil of Tiananmen Square. Wrongly dismissed as a lightweight by his critics, Jiang frequently confounded them. His effective partnership with Zhu Rongji, the articulate pro-market Premier, had reinforced China's path of strong economic growth. Jiang's description of China as a 'socialist market economy' was an indicator of his approach to economic management.

Consistent with maintaining the absolute dominance of the Chinese Communist Party, Jiang adopted a relatively benign attitude to Western nations, including Australia. In many ways he was the most surprising world leader I ever dealt with. I did not expect that the boss of the Chinese Communist Party and President of China would be a lover of classical Western music, especially Beethoven and Chopin. In addition, he enjoyed watching Western movies and had extensively viewed the classics of Hollywood's 'golden age' of the first half of the 20th century.

At the end of the usual cultural performance during the formal dinner, an ensemble trooped on stage to the tune of 'Auld Lange Syne'. I asked Jiang why that traditional Western piece had been used at a Chinese event. He replied by informing me that a film he especially recalled was *Waterloo Bridge*, and the tune had played at a particularly sentimental moment during that movie. His response astonished me, and because it was so specific, I accepted it without reservation. I did remember that movie, which starred Robert Taylor and Vivien Leigh, and was a romantic story set against the backdrop of London during World Wars I and II. My recall didn't include 'Auld Lang Syne', but a later check confirmed that Jiang's recollection was spot-on.

There could not have been anything contrived about this. Only an intense and genuine interest in the genre could have been the source of this detail. From my own experience, hosts at APEC meetings take a keen interest in the content of cultural presentations. This one certainly revealed the influences of Jiang Zemin.

The President's affinity for things Western did not stop at classical music and classic films. It extended to Shakespeare. Jiang exhibited a lively interest in and knowledge of the great bard's plays. When he discovered that my wife, Janette, had taught Shakespeare during her teaching career, he took to quoting passages from Shakespearean plays and asking Janette to identify both the play and the character involved. She thought it added a whole new dimension to formal dinners with my Chinese counterpart. He never caught her out!

Jiang Zemin had good conversational English. I was told that he had an even greater mastery of Russian. He was of that generation of Chinese that had spent a good deal of time in the old Soviet Union before the schism between the two powers began in 1960. While in the USSR he had studied engineering. He used an interpreter during formal one-on-one discussions, but impressed everyone at the Shanghai APEC by conducting all the plenary sessions in English. He even delivered his own speech in that language. Given recent events, it felt like a singular courtesy to the American President.

The early months of my government had seen rocky relations with China, including the fallout from Chinese missile testing in the Taiwan Strait, disputes over ministerial visits to Taiwan and the impact of a necessary cost-saving budget measure on some Chinese investments. A full-scale meeting with Jiang on the margins of the Manila APEC meeting late in 1996 had seen all our differences put on the table, with both sides resolving to focus on areas of common agreement as a way of improving the relationship.

At the end of the meeting, Jiang remarked, 'It's much better face to face,' and invited me to visit China the following year. His demeanour was that of a man who wanted a cooperative relationship between our two nations, despite our vastly different political systems. I was able to visit China the following Easter, and in the process establish a positive relationship with Jiang. He reciprocated with a successful visit to Australia in 1999.

By the time of the APEC summit in Brunei late in 2000, our relationship had made great strides. Jiang exhibited the same ease in dealing with democratic world leaders that I would later see in Shanghai. The Brunei gathering took place before the outcome of the closely contested Bush–Gore presidential election had been finally determined.

It would be Bill Clinton's last APEC, and understandably he was somewhat wistful. At the conclusion of the plenary session, I presumed to speak on behalf of all present in thanking Clinton for attending some seven APEC summits, and for his country's sponsorship of the group's goals more generally. Quite spontaneously, Jiang rose to second my remarks and spoke with equal warmth of our departing friend. There was nothing contrived. Jiang might have been a doctrinaire Chinese communist leader, but in this company he was very much a citizen of a wider world.

Looking back, Shanghai was something of a high-water mark in relations between China and the US. The declaration that emerged from that 2001 meeting carried a united anti-terrorism message from all the nations of the Asia-Pacific. China joined the World Trade Organization in December of that year. Jiang visited America the following year and stayed at the Bush ranch in Crawford, Texas.

China's rise since the early 2000s has been remarkable. Yet it has led to increasing tension with the US, and a growing strategic rivalry between the two nations in the Indo-Pacific region. Moreover, nothing can gainsay the suppression of open debate and the denial of fundamental human rights in that country. Minorities have been suppressed, of which Uighur Muslims and their treatment remains to this day a conspicuous example.

In other ways, though, China's rise has been not only good for China but also good for the world. During the past 20 years, more people have been lifted from poverty than during any equivalent time period since the Industrial

Revolution. China's economic expansion has been a major contributor to that. It has been the good news story of the early part of the 21st century.

Australia has been integral to this rapid industrialisation. Our fossil fuel exports have helped underpin Chinese growth. China has found in Australia a ready seller that honoured contracts, delivered on time, and had the very product that it wanted most: coking coal, ideal for high-quality steel manufacture. We have also been a dependable supplier of thermal coal for energy production, as well as iron ore and natural gas.

By 2002, I had come to appreciate that China was really warming to the idea of doing business with Australia. A huge natural gas sale to Guangdong Province by Australia's Northwest Shelf consortium came into prospect. China was seeking to diversify away from over-reliance on Middle Eastern sources. Northwest's main rival was a consortium involving BP and some Indonesian interests. Although this was a commercial transaction, to acknowledge the Asian way of doing things, I involved myself in the latter stages of the negotiations.

I knew that the leadership in Beijing would have the final say on the provincial government's decision. The Chinese Premier, Zhu Rongji, made it clear that, if the price were right, he wanted the contract to go to Australia. He even joked at one point that the Australians were trying harder, because their PM had come to China to lobby for the consortium, whereas the British had only sent their *deputy* PM, John Prescott, to speak for BP.

In the end, the Australian consortium won the contract. It was at that time Australia's largest ever export deal, comprising the supply of 3 million tonnes of liquefied natural gas per year for 25 years. The Chinese government was happy with the outcome, and in Australia it was widely seen as a consolidation of a hugely valuable trading relationship, and a vindication of our method of dealing with China.

Symbolism can never be a substitute for real progress in solving age-old political problems. Yet it is an essential part of relations between nations, and in some circumstances it can bear eloquent testimony to an important stage reached in those relations, even if no concessions are made, or ground conceded. Such was the case on the two successive days in October 2003 when joint sittings of the two houses of the Australian parliament were addressed respectively by President George W. Bush and Chinese President Hu Jintao.

Two American presidents had been given this honour before: President George H.W. Bush in 1992 and President Clinton in 1996. The serving President Bush was keen to visit Australia, and saw the opportunity of doing so immediately after the APEC meeting that year in Thailand. While at that meeting, we discussed his visit, and in particular his proposed address to the parliament. In a rather light-hearted fashion, he asked what kind of reception he might expect. I replied that it would be very warm, even if some of the Labor members might not clap all that loudly, because they disagreed with the invasion of Iraq. In similar vein, I told him that he might be heckled by 'a Green named Brown': a reference to Senator Bob Brown, leader of the Australian Greens and vocal critic of the Bush Administration. He thanked me for the warning.

It transpired that the Chinese President, who had a standing invitation to visit Australia, would be in Canberra at virtually the same time as President Bush. So it was very quickly decided to extend to him the same courtesy as that extended to George Bush. The Americans did not bat any eyelids at the 'double bill', even when it was established that the events would be on successive days. The Chinese were pleased to have the same treatment as the Americans. It was not lost on anybody that this was the first time the leader of an authoritarian country would be addressing the Australian parliament. The Chinese hoped to make the most of the event.

My warning to President Bush had been prescient. Bob Brown *did* interject, and the President fired back a retort to the effect of 'Isn't free speech terrific!' This drew a cheering response, even from some softly clapping ALP members. There were no more words from the senator.

Bob Brown's interjection had bothered the Chinese far more than it had President Bush. That afternoon, Chinese

Ambassador Madame Fu Ying, a professional in every way, called on Arthur Sinodinos, my chief of staff, and demanded an assurance that there would be no repetition of Brown's behaviour when the Chinese President spoke the following day. Arthur said that he could not give any such assurance, but promised Madame Fu that if Senator Brown transgressed the rules, he would be dealt with by the Speaker – knowing full well that those rules would not prevent Brown from interjecting. The President's speech went ahead, and fortunately Brown stayed silent.

There was something of a sequel. It was the custom when a visitor addressed a joint sitting to hold a large luncheon in the Great Hall in their honour. Naturally we offered that courtesy to both President Bush and President Hu. George Bush accepted and a large gathering ensued. Hu Jintao declined, but immediately indicated that on the following evening, after his address, he would be hosting a dinner at Canberra's Hyatt Hotel. Vague references to security concerns were invoked, but the reason was obvious: because they were hosting the dinner, the Chinese did not have to invite Bob Brown. Naturally I attended the dinner, which in every way followed the format for such occasions – minus Bob Brown!

The symbolism of this occasion was striking. On successive days, the respective leaders of the two most powerful countries in the world – one democratic, the other totalitarian – had spoken to a joint sitting of the

Australian parliament. To many observers, that was quite an achievement for Australia. Our links with the United States were deep and long-standing, steeped in the values we had in common. Those common values meant that we would always be closer to the US.

Our relationship with China was different, but rapidly growing. Within several years, China would become Australia's largest export destination and Chinese would replace Greek as the most widely spoken foreign language in our country. The Chinese component of our population was expanding rapidly. Now some 1.4 million Australians are of Chinese heritage.

It was in Australia's national interests that there be good relations with China. But this should never be at the expense of weakening our even closer ties with the US. For different reasons, and in vastly different ways, we needed to be close to both.

By 2003, some had begun to argue that, unavoidably, a choice would have to be made. In a powerfully symbolic manner, the twin addresses to the Australian parliament had demonstrated that we rejected such a concept. Strategic circumstances have altered since then, but it is still in Australia's national interests to remain deeply engaged with China.

At the time of writing there is no more perplexing foreign policy issue for Australia. Although China is our largest customer, and that reality played a major role in our avoidance of serious consequences from the GFC, the political and diplomatic aspects of our relationship have turned sour. The buoyancy of iron ore, coal and natural gas sales sustains an immensely valuable trading partnership, yet dark clouds are everywhere.

China has picked off other exports such as barley, wine and cotton, as well as employing delaying tactics in relation to some of our coal exports. Flimsy allegations of dumping have been made. A loquacious former Chinese ambassador has regularly attacked our foreign policy, listing questions that need to be addressed. Ministerial interaction has been virtually non-existent for more than two years. China has feigned offence at the call made by our previous Foreign Minister for an inquiry into the origins of COVID. There is no substance to the Chinese criticisms. There was nothing bellicose in the minister's statement, and it has not been followed by any anti-Chinese rhetoric.

Our perplexity at the chilly Chinese attitude of recent years is felt even more keenly because it has followed years during which Australia seemed to have found the right balance in its relations with both China and the US. As stated, we will always be closer to our great ally than to China, and I have never been reluctant to state this publicly. Yet I have always eschewed the proposition that at some point Australia will be forced to choose between those two powers.

Most of those who argue this way are wrongly of the view that, aided by a constantly growing economy and authoritarian efficiency in government, China is destined in time to surpass the United States and become the world's superpower. The rapid emergence of China has led many commentators to become mesmerised by the country. As a result, some of them have advocated that, in the national interest, Australia should edge closer to Beijing, even at the expense of our historic links with the Americans.

Not only does such thinking betray principle for the sake of short-term expediency, but it also demonstrates ignorance, wilful or otherwise, of two great impediments to China's seemingly unstoppable rise to the top. They are demography and the great governance dénouement.

China will grow old before it grows rich. Nothing can suppress this reality.[1] Those who are mesmerised by China should contemplate the circumstances that have attended the now abandoned one-child policy. Introduced in 1980 as an ill-judged demographic weapon against the potentially inflationary consequences of Chairman Deng Xiaoping's embrace of more market-inspired policies, it has been a failure of monumental proportions. It, more than anything else, has contributed to the grim demographic reality China now faces. Several years ago, it was liberalised to a two-child policy under certain circumstances. In mid-2021 that was further stretched to three children in particular situations.

These profound policy changes, in an area that is fundamental to long-term social stability and economic growth, reveal confused and contradictory policy reasoning at the pinnacle of the Chinese state. 'Demography is destiny' may be a hackneyed phrase, but it will have lasting resonance in the endless comparisons between the futures of the US and China.

China's is an ageing society. Changing that will be the slowest-turning ocean liner of the 21st century. The population of the United States, much wealthier as measured by per capita GDP, is far more advantageously placed in other ways too. Its fertility rate is 1.7, which contrasts favourably with China's, at 1.3.[2] Like so many other nations, China is condemned to a future in which a declining number of people of working age will be required to support a growing number in retirement. Yet China is much poorer than many countries with the equivalent problem, and its fertility rate is lower. The Chinese Academy of Social Sciences projects that if the current fertility rate continues, then China's population will halve to 700 million by 2100.[3] The old-age dependency ratio by then will be extremely onerous.

Looked at in isolation, population data have their limits in measuring economic and military power. China's economic growth has been impressive but should be kept in perspective. In 2018 the average value of China's output per worker was just 40 per cent of Japan's, 33 per cent of

Germany's and 26 per cent of the United States. Once again, to keep things in perspective, India's output per worker in 2018 was just 67 per cent of that in China, and 18 per cent of that in the US. Yet by 2027, India's population is expected to overtake China's. To add another population comparison, by 2050 America is projected to have added 41 million people through immigration, while China is forecast to lose 13 million as a result of emigration.[4] Openness has its rewards. This welter of statistics reminds us of just how important productivity or output per worker is to the economic growth of a nation.

The second great impediment China faces has to do with governance. For the past 40 years, China's leaders have sought to practise an unusual paradigm. It is based on the seemingly awkward marriage of economic liberalism and political authoritarianism. When Deng Xiaoping declared, in 1978, that henceforth China would embrace a market economy, he turned his back on decades of communist orthodoxy. China's economic performance since the 1949 takeover by the communists had been wretched. The Great Leap Forward and the Cultural Revolution had caused untold human misery and added nothing of value to China's economy. It would have been quite delusional for Deng and his colleagues to think that the command-economy model, followed with declining enthusiasm in Eastern Europe, was in any way a robust competitor for the capitalist West. The

Soviet economy was then creaking towards an existential threat, with frequent reliance on ad-hoc credits from Western sources.

It is only natural that people born into poverty who make the transition to relative affluence without the need for violent revolution will be more accepting of state direction in how to live their lives. They recall the less happy times, and give the prevailing political order some credit for their own improved socio-economic condition. That credit may often be well deserved. However, those born into relative comfort are more likely to assume that such comfort is the natural order of things, and be resentful of the state's attempts to monitor their behaviour and tell them how to live their lives.

Context is everything. Conservative estimates would place the population of China's growing middle class in the order of 400 million. An increasing proportion of this cohort has not experienced poverty. It is their parents who remember the harder days keenly. The popular view now is that young successful Chinese are in thrall to the state. President Xi Jinping has consolidated his grip on power. In the name of stamping out corruption he has eliminated political rivals (although a purge of some of the more venal among them was understandable). His aggressive international posture appeals to his compatriots and follows a path well trodden by leaders of newly emergent world powers.

It is beyond question that for some years now China and the United States have been the two most powerful nations on earth, both militarily and economically. But China's inescapable demographic challenge, coupled with the historic capacity of the United States to outcompete others through superior technology and higher productivity, should cause us to dispute the doomsday economic predictions that China will overtake America. Those ever ready to predict American decline relative to China should bear in mind the potential for an increasingly independent middle class to challenge authoritarianism. It may seem unlikely now, but so did the collapse of the Soviet Empire in the 1960s.

These observations are reinforced by the security reality China faces. It has the world's longest land border, which separates it from 14 neighbouring countries, and its main economic and population centres lie on the coast of a sea it does not control. It is preoccupied with several independence movements on its periphery, the potential collapse of North Korea, growing tensions with India, as well as territorial claims against several countries in the East and South China Seas.

Taiwan is the elephant in the room. The Chinese have always claimed that Taiwan is 'part of China', and since 1949 the Chinese aim has been to reintegrate Taiwan into the People's Republic of China. It is all too often overlooked that Beijing only ruled Taiwan for the brief period between

1945 and 1949. The island, formerly known as Formosa, was ceded to Japan as part of the peace settlement following the Sino-Japanese conflict of 1894 to 1895. Japanese sovereignty of Taiwan only ceased in 1945 on Japan's defeat at the end of World War II. After just five years, a protracted Chinese civil war ended in defeat for the Nationalists, who retreated to Taiwan and established it as the new territory of the Republic of China. This gives some context to communist China's historic claim.

For decades now, successive Australian governments, in line with governments in the US, have adhered to the one China policy, refusing to recognise Taiwan as a sovereign state. During President Nixon's historic visit to China in 1972, a communiqué was issued in Shanghai that has remained the basis of the current US policy. It said, inter alia: 'The United States acknowledges that all Chinese on either side of the Taiwan Strait maintain there is but one China and that Taiwan is a part of China. The United States Government does not challenge that position.'[5] The Shanghai Communiqué did not specifically say that the 'one China' in contemplation was the mainland governed from Beijing, but it did not disavow that interpretation either. Diplomatic representation of the nation-state type is now reserved for Beijing, so that Taiwan is denied membership of the UN and numerous other world bodies. In many other ways, though, Taiwan is treated as a separate country. For instance, the one China policy is flexible enough to accommodate the membership of China, Taiwan and Hong Kong in APEC, because that body is seen as a gathering of economies, not nations.

In May 2020, Pew Research found that 66 per cent of adults in Taiwan identified as Taiwanese and 28 per cent as both Chinese and Taiwanese, with only 4 per cent seeing themselves as just Chinese.[6] Such research is unlikely to influence what Beijing will ultimately do regarding Taiwan, nonetheless it confirms the strong sense of national identity among the Taiwanese. Theirs is a robust and prosperous nation, grown used to democracy and regular changes of government. No country has handled COVID-19 better. US trade with Taiwan exceeds that with either India or France. The recent aggressive Chinese treatment of Hong Kong will only have stiffened Taiwanese resolve. In a knock-down, drag-out fight, Taiwan would not be easy to subjugate. Moreover, a defeated and resentful Taiwan would prove a costly and resource-consuming Chinese province.

I regard it as highly unlikely that China will launch a conventional attack on Taiwan, largely because it fears a retaliatory response from the US that could well prove embarrassing. Military or other action short of a frontal strike is far more likely, particularly if it causes the US to agonise over how to respond. Neither the Americans nor the Chinese are likely to see profit in any kind of military engagement. Too much would ride on the perceived outcome.

Both sides of politics in Washington will continue to counsel Taiwan against provoking the mainland. In a thoughtful 2021 analysis, Robert D. Blackwill of the US Council on Foreign Relations and Virginia University Professor Philip Zelikow canvassed various possible courses of action the Chinese might take regarding Taiwan. They included conventional military action, and a naval blockade to raise the pressure on Taiwan. Blackwell and Zelikow pointed out that one of the consequences of any conflict between the US and China could be the freezing of financial flows between the two countries. That would be very painful for China, as it would block interest payments on Chinese holdings of US Treasury bonds, which, although recently scaled back, are still substantial.[7]

The recently announced AUKUS agreement between Australia, the United States and Britain, which aims to provide nuclear-powered submarines for Australia and underwrite other military cooperation between the three nations, is a clear earnest of their intention to provide a counterbalance to the growth of Chinese power in the Indo-Pacific. From the perspective of the current Australian government, the arrangement makes good sense, operationally, strategically and politically. Although their responses will be muted, other nations in the region will be pleased. China makes them uneasy. The Chinese will recognise the deal for what it is. It will be some time before Beijing decides on its long-term response, beyond the ritual attacks on provocative American behaviour. China's response may merely be to reinforce its current posture.

There is no sign that China's diplomatic sniping towards Australia will ease soon. In fact, it may be intensified because of AUKUS. Given Australia's now even closer links with the United States, and the quite sophisticated understanding the Chinese have of that relationship, I predict that Australia will remain something of a proxy punching bag in Chinese eyes. By endeavouring to provoke us, they hope to incite a reaction from the US, and because the real target is at one remove from their immediate thrusts, they feel safe in attacking Australia.

Amid all the diplomatic analysis, we Australians should not forget that the Chinese understand how valuable the economic links are between our two countries. For different reasons, we both need this trading relationship. Self-respecting pragmatism should always guide our approach to China. Fundamental beliefs should never be compromised, but schoolboy point-scoring should be shunned.

THE 2022 ELECTION

**Reflections on the outcome of the
May 2022 federal election and
the future of the Liberal Party**

The election on 21 May 2022 delivered the seventh change of government in Australia since World War II. It was the most grudging, unenthusiastic change of them all. Not only did Labor struggle to obtain an absolute majority, its primary vote at 32.75 per cent was the lowest of any incoming government in modern times. By comparison, the primary vote of the Coalition in 1996, when it won office, was 47.3 per cent. The ALP primary vote when Kevin Rudd defeated me in 2007 was 43.4 per cent.

There was no clear ideological message delivered by the election. To illustrate: the Greens had a good poll, winning three additional seats in the House of Representatives, and all in Queensland, which in other respects remained rock solid for the Coalition. The Nationals also performed well, retaining all their lower house MPs.

Earlier, I recalled that when first involved in politics I thought the electorate divided 40–40–20, and that in more recent times it had approached 30–30–40. I employed the latter comparison figuratively, but at the last election it came remarkably close to reality. Although exceeding that of the Labor Party, the Coalition's primary vote was a miserable 35.72 per cent.

There were sharply different voting patterns among the states. Queensland remained firm for the Coalition, where it retained 21 of its previously held 23 seats. Labor made no gains and lost one seat to the Greens. The two seats lost by the Liberals went to the Greens. There is only modified joy in that for Liberals and Nationals: the Greens are to the left of the ALP. Perhaps the LNP should reflect on the ill-wisdom of its decision in the last Queensland state election to preference a Green to defeat Jackie Trad (the left-wing former Labor Deputy Premier). Rank opportunism of that kind usually backfires. Did that cynical gesture confer some legitimacy on the Greens?

In contrast the Liberal Party lost four seats to Labor and one to a teal independent in Western Australia, where it suffered a state-wide swing against it of 10 per cent. Continuing the state analysis, the Liberal Party retained its two marginals in Tasmania. In South Australia the Liberals lost just Boothby, its only true marginal. The ALP gained seats from the Liberals in New South Wales and Victoria, but it was the havoc wreaked by the teals that did the most damage there. The maverick character of this poll was illustrated by the rejection of paratrooper Kristina Keneally in Fowler, and the Liberal, Melissa McIntosh, increasing her slim majority in Lindsay, an electorate that in 1996 had given birth to the Howard battlers. This praiseworthy effort was exceeded by Phillip Thompson in the Townsville-based seat of Herbert, who secured a swing of 3.31 per cent.

There was a portion of the electorate that had normally voted Liberal but, for a combination of reasons, was unhappy with the Morrison Government. The most frequently asserted reason for their disaffection was climate change. These voters, in electorates such as North Sydney and Kooyong, could not bring themselves to vote for Anthony Albanese but found in so-called 'teal' candidates a convenient repository for their discontented votes. In the process, in Kooyong, they ejected Josh Frydenberg, the former government's stand-out performer. He had not only been an excellent Treasurer, but a diligent local member.

I shall return to the teal phenomenon shortly. Suffice to say here that it is a mistake to see the vote for those candidates as composed only of disgruntled Liberals. It was a deliberate Labor tactic to depress its House of Representatives vote in those seats contested by teal candidates. To make my point, the Labor vote in Goldstein declined by 17.3 per cent, greater than the swing against Tim Wilson, the defeated former Liberal MP, of 12.3 per cent. Surely this leakage from Labor would have gone overwhelmingly to the teal victor, Zoe Daniel?

This assessment contains some massive generalisations but helps explain the low primary vote for the victorious Labor Party.

When Bob Hawke won in 1983 and I won in 1996, the electoral arithmetic in those cases saw a clear transfer of primary votes from Liberal to Labor and vice versa. That did not occur in May of this year.

It is often said that governments lose elections, oppositions do not win them. Perhaps the message out of Scott Morrison's 2019 victory should have been that the electorate's fear that Bill Shorten would increase taxation overcame the accumulated unhappiness of voters with divisions in Liberal ranks and other failures of the Coalition government, including that Scott Morrison himself had been the third Coalition Prime Minister in just six years. Perhaps 2019 was a case of an opposition losing an election. If that were the case, then Anthony Albanese's approach of repudiating the tax policies Bill Shorten had advocated at the 2019 election and being a 'small target' has proven to be extremely shrewd.

Critics said that Scott Morrison was personally unpopular. That is usually said of losing prime ministers.

It is an easy line, as an ex-PM is rarely seen as having a political future, and it suits those remaining in the fray for the blame to be borne by the defeated leader. Morrison's approval rating on the eve of the election was 41 per cent, against Kevin Rudd's approval rating on the eve of his defeat by Tony Abbott in 2013 of 33 per cent.

Morrison deserves enormous credit for having held the Liberal Party together after the turmoil of the Abbott–Turnbull years, and for his convincing victory in 2019. His leadership during the pandemic was impressive. Nothing can impeach a world-class ranking for Australia when it came to health outcomes, vaccination levels and the pace and extent of economic recovery from the pandemic. The incoming Albanese Government inherited a strong economy, with the lowest unemployment rate in 50 years.

Under Scott Morrison's leadership Australia concluded the AUKUS pact, the most significant defence arrangement since ANZUS. As well, our country joined the 'Quad', the Quadrilateral Security Dialogue between Australia, India, Japan and the US four durable long-standing democratic nations in the Asia–Pacific region. This a major hedge against Chinese expansionism.

Why then did the Coalition lose? Although Scott Morrison had been Prime Minister for only a little less than four years, the Coalition had been in power for nine years. That was longer than the Fraser Government, the Rudd–

Gillard–Rudd Government and, of course, the Whitlam Government. So, there was a time element involved.

Taking another approach, if one subdivides that nine-year period, then 2022 was Morrison's second election, and he could have suffered from the second election syndrome. Menzies, having won well in 1949, went backwards in 1951. Whitlam lost seats in 1974. So did Hawke in 1984. My large 1996 majority was heavily reduced in 1998. Fraser in 1977 held his huge margin from 1975, but the combatants were the same. Whitlam still led the ALP.

Looked at from either analysis, the public wanted the Coalition gone but had little enthusiasm for the government installed in its place.

The Liberal Party in Western Australia was reduced to just two seats at the last state election there. There is a widespread public perception that the party has yet to address the internal maladies, such as destructive factionalism, that caused such a humiliating rout. This contributed to an unexpectedly large swing against the Liberals at the federal election. In my opinion this tardiness did more damage to the Liberal brand in Western Australia than Morrison's short-lived dalliance with Clive Palmer's constitutional challenge.

The Liberal Party was not helped by delays and public antagonism surrounding preselections in New South Wales. The party in that state had gone through a tortuous process of establishing a new and more democratic system for choosing candidates. That new system should have been adhered to strictly. It wasn't. The notion that a sitting member of parliament deserves preferential treatment when it comes to choosing candidates is rightly unacceptable to ordinary party members.

If a sitting MP is challenged, that MP must be subjected to the normal processes for choosing candidates and not receive special protection.

There was a widespread claim that Scott Morrison was unpopular with women voters. At the time of writing, there is no post-election analysis publicly available on this issue. The former Prime Minister mishandled some issues specifically involving women. The most egregious was his parliamentary attack on Christine Holgate. She was a highly successful professional woman respected in the business community who, on any fair analysis, had not done anything wrong. It had the appearance of the Prime Minister using his office to bully Holgate into resigning her position. That was a damaging event.

Marise Payne, the Minister for Women, and once described by the Prime Minister as 'the Prime Minister for Women', failed to defend the Prime Minister against unjustified criticism regarding his attitude to women. This highlighted a conspicuous unwillingness of the government front bench to defend their leader against opposition and other attacks. I was often left with the feeling during the last 12 months of the government, that there were few Liberals saying anything on its behalf beyond the Prime Minister, the Treasurer and the Minister for Defence. I would add Greg Hunt, who spoke frequently and with persuasive detail on health issues.

Let me say here that it would be against the long-term cultural grain of the Liberal Party to introduce quotas so as to increase the party's female representation in parliament. That is a Labor approach. It is patronising and reeks of identity politics. Meritocracy is a basic Liberal value. Droves of able, dedicated women in the party would strongly oppose them. Calls for quotas often come from certain Liberals who believe that the party's future lies in being as indistinguishable as possible from the Labor Party. The shadow cabinet has a large female component.

The considerations I have canvassed above all played a role in the Coalition's defeat. But that would not have been enough to deny the Liberal and National Parties victory against a Labor Party that manifestly failed to enthuse and was led by a gaffe-prone man who conducted a poor campaign.

The single largest failure of the Coalition was that it did not present to the Australian people a clear policy manifesto for the future. If, as I believe, politics is, above everything else, a battle of ideas, then beyond the quite imaginative housing policy released a week before the election, there was no stark policy theme highlighting differences between the then government and opposition.

The Liberals and Nationals kept saying that it was a clear choice, but never spelt out what the choices were, beyond the generalisations that they were superior on economic management and national security.

In 2019 the Coalition could argue convincingly that the Labor Party would undermine Australia's fossil fuel industries, which contribute so much to our national wealth. This powerful policy weapon was largely destroyed by our Glasgow commitment. The public perception was that the differences between Labor and the Coalition on climate change had markedly diminished. It could well be salutary to consider that the National Party, with some in its ranks having argued against net zero by 2050, did not lose any seats.

The Coalition was left asserting that it should be re-elected on the strength of its past record on economic management and national security. It had an impressive argument to mount, notwithstanding the tendency of the electorate to bank past achievements and ask for more. There was also the danger that black swan events might sabotage that approach. That proved to be the case with the double whammy of the 5.1 per cent inflation figure just two weeks before the poll and, inevitably, the rise in interest rates that followed.

Even more damaging was the agreement between China and the Solomon Islands. It came from nowhere and must have shaken confidence in the government's credentials in this area.

Since the early 1980s the Liberal Party has been seen as the party of economic reform. A proper understanding of the Hawke and Keating Governments is that many of the economic policies they implemented had been promoted by the Liberals. As examples, I cite financial deregulation, tariff reductions and privatisation. They were good policies and those Labor governments deserved credit for pursuing them, notwithstanding ALP attacks on the Liberal Party when it first propounded them. They were all adopted with Coalition support. That support removed any political pain that might otherwise have occurred, particularly given that they overturned the conventional wisdom of decades.

The Coalition won office in 1996 promising an industrial-relations shake-up, further privatisation, a family tax benefit plan and other economic reforms (hardly the 'small target' strategy so inaccurately attached to the Liberal–National campaign for that election). The 1998 election was dominated by the GST-inspired new tax system, the largest overhaul of our taxation system since World War II.

The 2001 election saw a continuation, as the ALP opposition promised a 'rollback' of elements of the GST. The Coalition's victory in 2004 was in part attributable to the electorate's acceptance that its policies were more likely to produce lower interest rates.

Kevin Rudd defeated my government in 2007. Much of the debate centred on WorkChoices and whether Australia should ratify the Kyoto Protocol on reduced greenhouse gas emissions. The Coalition's stance on them was grounded in economic considerations. We lost the argument on both issues. The Liberal and National Parties in 2007 also proposed a major restructuring of the income tax scales, which Labor essentially adopted.

The 2010 and 2013 elections, fought from opposition by the Coalition, focused heavily on border protection and climate change, with the electorate seeing a clear choice between the ALP and the Liberals. Labor, in government after 2007, had not proved to be good economic managers, and in each of those elections the Coalition won the argument that it was a superior when it came to running the economy.

It was instructive that in 2016 the Coalition, then in government, did not lay out further economic reforms and lost 14 seats. In hindsight there was a warning in this for the Liberals, which they clearly did not heed.

Even in those cases, such as 2007, when the public appeared to have rejected our principal economic plan for the future – WorkChoices – the Coalition could claim to have presented a clear policy prescription.

Beyond Tony Abbott's courageous initiative of the Australian Building and Construction Industry Commission, the Coalition has gone to water on industrial relations for more than a decade. If the Albanese Government attempts to dismantle this commission, the Liberal and National Parties should fight for its retention.

For the past five years the Coalition baulked at any major economic reform, preferring to rely on the generalised claim, certainly valid, that it has been a better economic manager in government. Such an approach always had a shelf life, and it was reached at the last election. The Liberal and National Parties must present a substantial economic plan at the next election. At a minimum, taxation and industrial relations must be addressed in that plan. But it should go beyond those issues.

The most talked-about feature of the campaign was the victory of self-styled independents in the six previously held Liberal electorates of Wentworth, North Sydney and Mackellar in Sydney; Curtin in Western Australia; and Kooyong and Goldstein in Melbourne. They joined like-minded Zali Stegall, who won Warringah from Tony Abbott in 2019. They had a common source for some of their funding and there was clear coordination of campaign techniques among them as a group.

They reacted adversely to my description of them as 'anti-Liberal'. Yet the evidence was plain to see. None of their ilk nominated against a Labor MP. Their policy priorities were climate change and an anti- corruption commission. The Coalition and Labor had largely similar positions on both of these issues. Although the Liberals had a detailed measure prepared for such a commission, it suffered, politically, from not having presented the Bill to parliament.

For some reason I cannot fathom, Coalition governments after mine have not followed the practice my government did of presenting legislation on contentious issues likely to be rejected by Labor to the Senate, and seeing it accepted or voted down there. The Howard Government, for example, tried on numerous occasions to win Senate approval for changes to unfair dismissal laws, finally having them accepted only after it had secured a majority in the upper house at the 2004 election. The small business community, which keenly desired the changes, was left in no doubt about our stance on the issue. By contrast, the Morrison Government never forced the opposition to say yes or no in parliament to its preferred model for the commission. Thus, it was reduced to saying that it had a 300-page Bill ready if only the opposition would come on board. It would have been more convincing if the PM had been able to say that our Bill had been voted down in the Senate by Labor and the Greens.

The Coalition took far too long to put together its Religious Discrimination Bill and went to the polls in some disarray on the issue. This disappointed many traditional

Liberal supporters. If this matter had been addressed sooner and internal differences resolved, the Australian Christian Lobby (ACL) may not have felt compelled to campaign against some Liberal MPs who had voted in parliament for a measure the ACL saw as diminishing the right of faith-based schools to maintain the religious ethos of their respective schools. This specific issue was of understandable concern to the ACL, a body which certainly had not exhibited any inherent hostility to the Coalition.

As I have written earlier, I remain an agnostic on climate change. That seems a minority position at present. What should not be a minority position is the importance of our fossil fuel exports to the future prosperity of our nation. A too hasty abandonment of gas and coal in pursuit of renewables could seriously damage our economy. Yet, the pressure to do precisely that has risen markedly as a result of the May election. The parliament now has many more climate-change zealots. There are 12 Greens in the Senate, and four in the House of Representatives. The six teals elected in May join Zali Stegall as MPs whose principal raison d'être is stronger action on climate change. Given that the ALP and the Greens together comprise half of the Senate of 76, and that their policies on many issues closely align, it is not hard to see the Albanese Government giving ground to the Greens on climate change in return for Senate support on a range of other issues.

In the days following the election, the most encouraging statement made by Peter Dutton was, 'I'm not a moderate, nor am I a conservative. I am a Liberal.' It is a sentiment I warmly endorse. The broad church of which I have often spoken appropriately describes the party I joined 65 years ago. It is the custodian of both the classical liberal and the conservative traditions. It performs best when that understanding infuses its policy-making and its choice of candidates.

For some years now factionalism has poisoned the Liberal Party's body politic. A successful government in South Australia, which had restored the health of that state's economy, was recently ejected after only one term partly because it was seen as bitterly divided along factional lines. In 2018 Steven Marshall led the Liberals to victory after 16 years in opposition and governed well. Despite a slender majority, several of his MPs, for a variety of reasons – which included factional differences – ended up leaving the party, thus putting the Marshall Government into a minority position.

This followed something of a South Australian Liberal pattern. Largely forgotten now, but in the 1990s Dean Brown – a self-proclaimed moderate – scored a big win for the Liberal Party after years of Labor rule. During his first term he was deposed in favour of John Olsen, from the more conservative side of the party. Brown and Olsen had stood against each other for party leadership in opposition. My preference then had been Olsen, but Brown won the leadership ballot, and later an overwhelming electoral victory. He should have been left there. It was foolish for the party to have done otherwise. Much to his credit John Olsen stayed around to help the Liberals, long after his parliamentary days ended. He currently serves as Federal President of the party.

In New South Wales the party has been riven by factional disputes, which have owed precious little to policy differences, but represent the ongoing struggle between what can only be called rival preferment cooperatives. As I have already noted elsewhere, all too often preselections for safe Liberal seats are contests between 'one of ours' or 'one of theirs'. Merit is often an also-ran.

It is fanciful to imagine that factionalism will ever totally disappear, and the Liberal Party's long-term health is not dependent on that occurring. But unless the increasing tendency for factions to operate as parties within a party is reversed, enduring damage will be done to the party's broad appeal. To use a time-honoured expression, there is blame on both sides.

To say the least, there has been a breakdown in civility within the Liberal Party, and often driven by factional rivals. Matt Kean, the Treasurer in the New South Wales Liberal government and a declared moderate/progressive identity, from time to time attacked the Morrison Government for not going far enough on climate change. His rogue intervention in calling for the removal of the federal Liberal candidate for Warringah, Katherine Deves, occurred after the last election campaign had started, was completely unrelated to his ministerial responsibilities, and was quite destabilising to the Warringah campaign.

Rampant factionalism had cost the Coalition dearly at the 2010 election. The most marginally held Labor seat in Australia after the Howard Government's defeat in 2007 was Robertson on the Central Coast of New South Wales. Jim Lloyd, a minister in my government, lost the seat by only 184 votes. He remained popular in the electorate, having recently represented the area for 12 years, and was willing to run again, but his endorsement was bitterly opposed by the so-called right-wing group, who dominated the Liberal branches in Robertson.

Lloyd saw the writing on the wall and did not nominate. The chosen Liberal candidate lost to Labor's Deborah O'Neill in an election that saw many less-vulnerable ALP seats go to the Liberals. If Robertson had fallen to the Liberal Party, the ALP would have had fewer seats than the Coalition and very likely would not have been able to form the minority Gillard Government. Jim Lloyd sat fairly in the centre of the Liberal Party and had run a small business before entering parliament. He was out of central casting for that electorate.

In the climate of the times, he would have taken back Robertson for the Liberals.

At the time of writing, it is early days for both the government and the opposition. Peter Dutton showed boldness and skill in composing his shadow ministry. He will need to oversee policy development through the next three years so that the Coalition has a clear program for the electorate.

That program must echo the values of the Liberal Party. It must reflect respect for the individual, support for free enterprise, and a belief that strong families not only provide emotional harbour for individuals, but constitute the most efficient social-welfare system mankind has ever devised. It should also reaffirm Australia's alignment with the democratic world and give unflinching support to the international liberal order.

On a more specific note, it should identify nuclear power as fundamental to our nation's energy future. Elsewhere I have written extensively about this. Liberals are constantly told that the science should be obeyed on climate change. If that be the case, then nuclear power, its costs, the timescales involved and the safeguards required must be front and centre of the energy debate. The science is certainly in on nuclear power being a clean, reliable source of baseload power.

Can I conclude on a cultural note? Earlier I wrote that common values bind nations more tightly together than anything else. The same applies to political parties and their supporters. In recent years the Liberal Party has disappointed many of its traditional supporters by being slow to attack the emergence of faddish ideas in areas such as education, forays into supposedly gender-neutral language in the public service, and other excursions into political correctness, all in the name of 'diversity' or 'equality'. Timidity can best describe the reactions of both Federal and state Coalition governments to many of these developments. The muted response to the Safe Schools push comes to mind.

My critics will say 'no big deal'. It is really. The concern of people about what they see as undermining traditional attitudes mounts over time. In isolation each concern may not appear significant, but together they build to a level of anger. Those who think such concerns are no more than obsessing about the trivial often dismiss the people who raise them with a blithe 'Those conservatives have got nowhere to go.'

At the May election some of those conservatives did find somewhere else to go, and the exodus helped remove a Liberal government.

ENDNOTES

INTRODUCTION

1   High Court of Australia, *Mabo v Queensland (No 2)*, 1992, staging.hcourt.gov.au/assets/publications/judgments/1992/016- -MABO_AND_OTHERS_v._QUEENSLAND_(No._2)-- (1992)_175_CLR_1.html, decision of Toohey J, para 16.

2   *Ibid*, decision of Brennan J, paras 24, 28, 35 33, 35 and 49; decision of Dean and Gaudron JJ, paras 2 and 3; and decision of Toohey J, para 16.

3   Australian Curriculum, Assessment and Reporting Authority (ACARA), 'National Report on Schooling in Australia 2019', www.acara.edu.au/reporting/national-report-on-schooling-in-australia; National Center for Education Statistics (US), 'Digest of Education Statistics', nces.ed.gov/programs/digest/current_ tables.asp; Explore Education Statistics (UK), 'Education and Training Statistics for the UK: 2020', explore-education-statistics.service.gov.uk/find-statistics/education-and-training-statistics-for-the-uk/2020; Statistics Canada, 'Vast majority of students attended public schools prior to the pandemic', *The Daily*, 15 October 2021, www150.statcan.gc.ca/n1/daily-quotidien/201015/dq201015a-eng.htm.

The Mob: How Dare They!

1   John Howard, *Long Live the Nation-State*, 19 November 2015, *National Review*, www.nationalreview.com/magazine/2015/11/19/long-live-nation-state/.

2   David Goodhart, *The Road to Somewhere: The Populist Revolt and the Future of Politics*, Hurst Publishers, 2017.

3   Ingrid van Biezen and Thomas Poguntke, 'The Decline of Membership-based Politics', *Party Politics*, Vol 20(2), 2014, pp 205–216.

Bowling Alone

1   Robert Putnam, *Bowling Alone: The Collapse and Revival of American Community*, New York: Simon & Schuster, 2000.

2   Robert Putnam, 'Who Killed Civic America?', *Prospect*, 20 March 1996, www.prospectmagazine.co.uk/magazine/whokilledcivicamerica.

3   Geoff Gilfillan and Chris McGann, 'Trends in Union Membership in Australia', Parliament of Australia, 15 October 2018, www.aph.gov.au/About_Parliament/Parliamentary_Departments/Parliamentary_Library/pubs/rp/rp1819/UnionMembership; OECD, 'Trade Union Dataset', stats.oecd.org/Index.aspx?DataSetCode=TUD.

Choosing the Leader

1   'A Good Government was Losing its Way, says Gillard', *Sydney Morning Herald*, 24 June 2010, www.smh.com.au/national/a-good-government-was-losing-its-way-says-gillard-20100624-z10k.html.

The Broad Church

1   Manning Clark, Lionel Murphy obituary, *Sydney Morning Herald*, 30 October 1986, p 2.

Bipartisanship: A One-way Street

1   Tom Frame, *The Desire for Change, 2004–2007: The Howard Government Volume IV*, NewSouth Publishing, Sydney, 2021, pp 365–366.

2   Malcolm Fraser, 'Election Speeches 1975', 27 November 1975, Melbourne, electionspeeches.moadoph.gov.au/speeches/1975-malcolm-fraser.

3   Ronald Reagan, 'Inaugural Address', 20 January 1981, Washington, www.reaganfoundation.org/ronald-reagan/reagan-quotes-speeches/inaugural-address-2/.

4   Ian Macfarlane, 'Lecture 3: Reform and Deregulation', *Boyer Lectures* 2006, www.abc.net.au/radionational/programs/boyerlectures/lecture-3-reform-and-deregulation/3353122.

5   '33 MPs Seek Tariff Cuts', *Canberra Times*, 7 December 1981.

6   Paul Keating, 'Press Statement by Paul Keating, Shadow Treasurer: "Mr Howard & Foreign Bank Entry"', 26 January 1983, Parliament of Australia, House of Representatives.

7   Terry McCrann, 'Two Sleepers Lie behind Keating's Open Door', *The Age*, 11 September 1984 (quoting Paul Keating, shadow treasurer, February 1983).

8   Ross Gittins, *Sydney Morning Herald*, 12 September 1984.

Constitutional Change

1   *Commonwealth of Australia Constitution Act 1900*, 9 July 1900, www.legislation.gov.uk/ukpga/Vict/63-64/12/introduction/enacted.

2   Supreme Court of the United States, *Obergefell v Hodges*, 2015, dissenting opinion of Roberts CJ, medium.com/@e/dissenting-opinion-of-justice-john-c-roberts-f5e2ab4f1349.

Climate Change and Nuclear Power

1   'Another Ice Age?', *Time Magazine*, 24 June 1974, content.time.com/time/subscriber/article/0,33009,944914,00.html.

2   Bjorn Lomborg, 'Do the Maths for the Real Story on Climate Disasters', *The Australian*, 11 September 2021, www.theaustralian.com.au/inquirer/do-the-maths-for-the-real-story-on-climate-disasters/news-story/3599246ae2ca9f5de31eb4a5abf5240d.

3   Marcos Quijal-Zamorano, 'Seasonality Reversal of Temperature Attributable Mortality Projections due to Previously Unobserved Extreme Heat in Europe', *The Lancet: Planetary Health*, Vol 5(9), 1 September 2021, www.thelancet.com/journals/lanplh/article/PIIS2542-5196(21)00211-4/fulltext#gr1.

4   William Nordhaus, *The Challenge of Global Warming: Economic Models and Environmental Policy*, Yale University, New Haven, 24 June 2007, www.econ.yale. edu/~nordhaus/homepage/OldWebFiles/DICEGAMS/dice_ mss_072407_all.pdf.
5   Nigel Lawson, *An Appeal to Reason: A Cool Look at Global Warming*, Overlook Duckworth, Peter Mayer Publishers Inc, New York, 2008, p 36.
6   Prime Ministerial Task Group on Emissions Trading, *Report of the Task Group on Emissions Trading*, 31 May 2007, Department of Prime Minister and Cabinet, apo.org.au/sites/ default/files/resource-files/2007-06/apo-nid968.pdf.

Long May She Reign!
1   Parliament of Australia, *Powers and Functions of the Governor-General: Prerogative powers*, www.aph.gov. au/About_Parliament/House_of_Representatives/Powers_ practice_and_procedure/practice5/chapter1#an38.

The Great Australian Dream
1   ABS, 3301.0 – Births, Australia, 2006, 29 October 2007, www.abs.gov.au/ausstats/abs@.nsf/mediareleasesbytitle/38 00BBDF8F4AA919CA257380001AAD5C?OpenDocumen t#:~:text=110%2F2007-,Fertility%20statistics%20for%20 2006%20now%20available%3A%20ABS,of%20Statistics%20 (ABS)%20today; and 'Australian Fertility Rate Hits Record Low', 8 December 2021, www.abs.gov.au/media-centre/media-releases/australian-fertility-rate-hits-record-low.

9/11: Twenty-one Years On
1   John Howard, Press Conference – Ambassador's Residence, Washington DC, 12 September 2001, Department of the Prime Minister and Cabinet, pmtranscripts.pmc.gov.au/release/ transcript-11804.
2   'Most Reinforce Decision on Troops', *The Australian*, 31 October 2001.

3   Donald Rumsfeld, *Known and Unknown: A Memoir*, Penguin, 2011, p 682.
4   *Ibid*, p 683.
5   John Howard, 'Transcript of Press Conference with the Prime Minister: Parliament House, Canberra: Troop Deployment to Afghanistan, Telstra, Rau Family', 13 July 2005, Parliament of Australia.
6   Joel Fitzgibbon, 'Speech by the Minister for Defence to the Brookings Institution', 16 July 2008, Washington DC, parlinfo.aph.gov.au/parlInfo/search/display/display. w3p;query=Id:%22media/pressrel/1R0R6%22.
7   Donald Rumsfeld, *op cit*, p 682.
8   George Bush, 'Address to the United Nations General Assembly in New York City', 12 September 2002, www. govinfo.gov/content/pkg/PPP-2002-book2/html/PPP-2002-book2-doc-pg1572.htm.
9   House of Representatives Committees, *Inquiry into Intelligence of Iraq's Weapons of Mass Destruction (WMD)*, Appendix F, Parliament of Australia, 1 March 2004, www. aph.gov.au/parliamentary_business/committees/house_of_representatives_committees?url=pjcaad/wmd/report.htm.
10   Mark Bowden, *The Finish: The Killing of Osama Bin Laden*, 2012, Thorndike Press, p 258.
11   Robert W. Gates, *Exercise of Power: American Failures, Successes, and a New Path Forward in the Post–Cold War World*, Knopf, 2020, p 196.

The China Dilemma
1   John Kemp, 'China's Productivity More Important than its Ageing Population', Reuters, 12 May 2021, www.reuters.com/ business/energy/chinas-productivity-more-important-than-its-ageing-population-kemp-2021-05-12/; Organisation for Economic Co-operation and Development (OECD), 'Ageing and Demographic Change: Fiscal Challenges and Inclusive Growth in Ageing Societies', www.oecd.org/economy/ageing-inclusive-growth/; 'Demographic Trends', OECD iLibrary,

www.oecd-ilibrary.org/sites/c05578aa-en/index.html?itemId=/
content/component/c05578aa-en.

2   National Center for Health Statistics (US), 'Births:
     Provisional Data for 2019', *Vital Statistics Rapid Release*,
     Report No 8, May 2020, www.cdc.gov/nchs/data/vsrr/
     vsrr-8-508.pdf; Helen Gao, 'China's Generation of Only
     Children Wants the Same for their Kids', *Foreign Policy*,
     4 November 2021, foreignpolicy.com/2021/11/04/china-one-
     child-policy-fertility-rates/#:~:text=China's%20fertility%20
     rate%E2%80%94the%20number,2.2%20for%20India%20
     in%202020.

3   'China's Population is about to Shrink for the First Time
     since the Great Famine Struck 60 Years Ago. Here's What
     it Means for the World', *The Conversation*, 30 May2022,
     theconversation.com/chinas-population-is-about-to-shrink-
     for-the-first-time-since-the-great-famine-struck-60-years-ago-
     heres-what-it-means-for-the-world-176377.

4   Kemp, *op cit*.

5   Office of the Historian, *Foreign Relations of the United States,
     1969–1976*, Volume XVII, China, 1969–1972 history.state.
     gov/historicaldocuments/frus1969-76v17/d203.

6   Kat Devlin and Christine Huang, *In Taiwan, Views of
     Mainland China Mostly Negative* Pew Research Center,
     12 May 2020, www.pewresearch.org/global/2020/05/12/in-
     taiwan-views-of-mainland-china-mostly-negative/.

7   Robert D Blackwell and Philip Zelikow, *United-States, China
     and Taiwan: A Strategy to Prevent War*, Council on Foreign
     Relations, February 2021, www.cfr.org/report/united-states-
     china-and-taiwan-strategy-prevent-war.

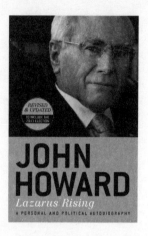

John Howard's autobiography, *Lazarus Rising*, is the best-selling Australian political memoir. In his account from boyhood to world stage, he talks about his love of family, his rollercoaster ride to the Lodge and how – as Prime Minister – he managed a strongly growing Australian economy and led Australia's war on terrorism. Drawing on his deep interest in history, he paints a fascinating picture of a changing Australia.

In this edition, fully updated to take into account the victory of the Coalition in the 2013 election, Howard analyses the crucial years between the 2010 election, which gave rise to the minority government of Julia Gillard, and the consequent unprecedented and destabilising leadership struggles within the Labor Party. He discusses the significance of Tony Abbott's achievements in defeating the Labor government in 2013, and provides a masterful summary of the legacy of the Rudd–Gillard years for Australia. *Lazarus Rising* is essential reading for all followers of politics.

'John Howard has written a magisterial autobiography, compulsively readable in its way' *The Weekend Australian*

'Underneath Howard's plain political style lies an excellent communicator. His capacity to express his thoughts clearly, calmly and simply shines through' *Sydney Morning Herald*

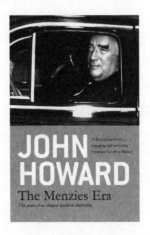

The monumental Sir Robert Menzies held power for a total of over 18 years, making him the longest serving Australian Prime Minister. During his second term as Prime Minister, which lasted more than 16 years – by far the longest unbroken tenure in that office – Menzies dominated Australian politics like no one else has ever done before or since.

The Menzies era saw huge economic growth, social change and considerable political turmoil, and laid the foundations for modern Australia.

Covering the impact of the great Labor split of 1955, as well as the recovery of the Labor Party under Whitlam's leadership in the late 1960s, and the impact of the Vietnam War on Australian politics, this account offers an assessment of the man and the times. John Howard was only ten when Menzies rose to power, and in young adulthood when the Menzies era ended, but he saw Menzies as an inspiration and role model. Howard's insights and thoughtful analysis make this a fascinating, highly significant book.

'John Howard, in this important book, takes us back to an era when there was a proper language in which to speak about such things. It's time travel' Clive James, *Times Literary Supplement*

'Engaging and revealing ... like a torchlight shone from an unexpected angle' Geoffrey Blainey, *Weekend Australian*